Read·n·Grow
PICTURE BIBLE

Edited by Libby Weed, Illustrated by Jim Padgett

Sweet Publishing
Fort Worth, Texas

Library of Congress Catalog Card Number 84-051093
ISBN 0-8344-0124-X

CONTENTS

JESUS TEACHES AND HEALS

JESUS' LAST WEEK

THE CHURCH BEGINS

PAUL'S MISSIONARY JOURNEYS

NEW TESTAMENT WRITINGS

In the Beginning

1 The very first story in the Bible tells how God made the world and everything in it. "In the beginning God made the heavens and earth."

2 At first the earth had no shape and was empty. Everything was dark. But the Spirit of God was there.

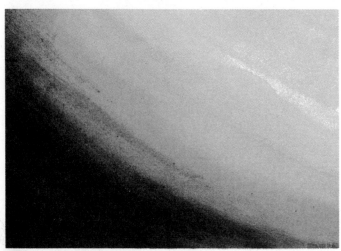

3 God said, "Let there be light," and there was light. Then God separated the light and the dark. He called the light "day" and the dark "night." This was what God did on the first day.

4 Next God separated the waters and put a space between them. God called this space the "sky." This was the second day.

5 On the third day God caused the waters to be gathered so that dry ground would appear. God called the dry ground "land" and he called the gathered waters "seas."

6 That same day God said, "Let the land be filled with trees and plants," and it was. All the plants made seeds, and all the trees had fruit with seeds so that there would always be plants and trees.

7 On the fourth day God made lights in the sky—the sun and the moon and the stars. These made light for the earth. The sun was for the day and the moon and stars for the night.

8 Next God caused the seas to be filled with fish and other living things. God also made birds which could fly in the sky. This was the fifth day of creation.

9 On the sixth day God made the animals that live on the land. He made cattle and wild animals that crawl on the ground.

10 There were no farm crops yet, because there were no people to grow them. And there was no rain yet. Plants and trees got their water from mists that came up from the ground.

11 When God finished making all these things, he looked at them and was pleased. Everything he had made was very good.

12 But God was not yet finished. Before the sixth day ended God planned to make something else, something very important.

The Creation of Man and Woman

1 God had created a beautiful earth, filled with fish and birds and all kinds of animals. Now he was ready to make something very special—people!

2 God said, "Let us make man in our image, so he will be like us." He made a man (Adam) from the dust of the ground and breathed into his nostrils the breath of life. So Adam became a living person.

3 Now the Lord had planted a garden in Eden. There were many trees of all kinds in the garden. They were very beautiful and their fruit was delicious.

4 In the middle of the garden were two special trees—the tree of life and the tree of the knowledge of good and evil.

5 The Lord God took Adam and put him in the garden of Eden. He told him to care for the garden.

6 God allowed Adam to eat the fruit of all the trees in the garden—except one! God warned Adam not to eat from the tree of the knowledge of good and evil. "If you do, you will surely die," God said.

7 Now the Lord God said, "It is not good for Adam to be alone." So God decided to make a helper who would be just right for Adam.

8 God brought to Adam all the birds and animals he had made so Adam could give them names. But none of these creatures was just right to be Adam's helper.

9 So God caused Adam to fall into a deep sleep. Then God took a rib from Adam's side and made a woman (Eve) from the rib.

10 When Adam woke up and saw the woman, he said, "This is bone of my bones and flesh of my flesh." (That is why a man leaves his father and mother and is joined to his wife. The two of them become as one.)

11 God told Adam and Eve to have many children so that people would live all over the earth. He also told them that he was putting them in charge of all the fish and birds and animals of the earth.

12 When God finished making man and woman on the sixth day, his work was completed. On the seventh day God rested. He made the seventh a holy day because on that day his creation was complete.

Sin Enters the World

1 God had put Adam and Eve in the garden of Eden to take care of it. But trouble soon appeared—in the form of a clever animal called a serpent.

2 Now the serpent was the most tricky of all the animals on the earth. The serpent asked Eve, "Did God really say that you must not eat from any tree in the garden?"

3 Eve answered, "We may eat the fruit of any tree in the garden except the tree in the middle of it. God told us not to eat from it or even touch it. If we do, we will die."

4 But the serpent said, "That's not true! You won't die! God just said that because he knows that when you eat it you will be like him, knowing good and evil."

5 Then Eve thought how good the fruit of the tree looked and how wonderful it would be to be as wise as God. So she took some of the fruit and ate it. She gave some to Adam and he ate it, too.

6 As soon as they had eaten it, they both understood for the first time that they were naked. So they sewed some fig leaves together to make coverings for their bodies.

7 That evening when they heard the Lord God walking in the garden, they hid among the trees. Adam finally told God that they had hidden because they were naked and afraid.

8 Adam confessed he had eaten the forbidden fruit, but he blamed it on his wife Eve. Eve put the blame on the serpent. She said the serpent had tricked her into eating it.

9 Then God said to the serpent, "As punishment, from now on you will have to crawl on your belly in the dust. And your kind will be the enemies of people forever."

10 Next God spoke to the woman. "You will have great pain when you give birth to your children," he said. "Even so you will still want your husband, and he will have control over you."

11 To Adam God said, "You will have to work hard and sweat to make the ground produce enough food. You will work until you die. You were made from the dust of the ground and you will become dust again!"

12 God made Adam and Eve leave the garden. He put guards there so that no one could eat from the tree of life and live forever. All this trouble happened because of sin. And more trouble lay ahead.

Cain and Abel

1 Because of their sin, Adam and Eve could no longer live in the garden of Eden. The sin they had brought into the world would cause even more trouble later.

2 Adam and Eve had two sons. They named the first son Cain. The second they named Abel.

3 As time passed, the boys grew up. Abel became a shepherd. His older brother, Cain, became a farmer.

4 One day the two sons brought gifts to the Lord. Gifts for God are often called "sacrifices" or "offerings." Cain's offering was something he had grown in the fields, and Abel's was a little lamb.

5 The Lord was pleased with Abel's offering. But he was not pleased with the offering which Cain brought.

6 This made Cain very angry.

7 Then the Lord said to Cain, "Why are you so angry? If you had done the right thing, I would have been pleased with you, too. Sin is trying to get the best of you—so watch out!"

8 But Cain paid no attention to the Lord's warning. One day while Cain and Abel were out in the fields, Cain attacked Abel and killed him.

9 The the Lord said to Cain, "Where is your brother Abel?" "How should I know?" Cain replied angrily. "Am I supposed to be taking care of my brother?"

10 But the Lord said, "Cain, I know you have murdered your brother. Because of that you will not be able to get the ground to grow anything. You will be a homeless wanderer!"

11 Cain cried, "This punishment is too much! I won't be able to stand it. I have to go away from this land and from you—and whoever sees me will kill me!"

12 So the Lord put a mark on Cain so no one would kill him. Then Cain went away and lived in the land of Nod, which means "Wandering." Thus Cain was punished for his sin.

God Sends a Flood

1 After Cain killed his brother Abel and was sent away, Adam and Eve had many other children.

2 In those days people lived to be very, very old. But no matter how long people lived, everyone had to die sooner or later. No one could escape death forever.

3 There was a man named Noah living then. He was an old man with three sons. Their names were Shem, Ham, and Japheth.

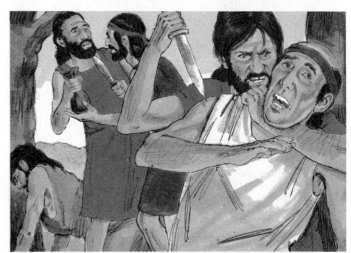

4 People were doing very evil things in Noah's day. It seemed as though the more people there were, the more wicked people became.

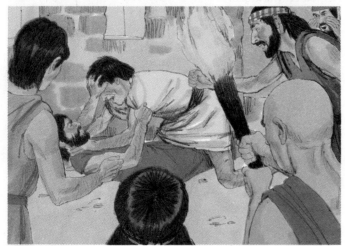

5 Finally, people's wickedness became so great that God was sorry he had ever made them. He decided to destroy all the people living on the earth who did not obey him.

6 However, there was one man whom God planned to save—Noah. He was the only person living in those days who was not evil. Noah was a good man who loved God.

7 Because God was pleased with Noah, he told Noah about his plan. "I will bring a flood upon the earth," God said, "to destroy all living things." Noah was to have a part in God's plan.

8 God told Noah to build a huge boat, called an ark. God told Noah exactly how he wanted the ark built.

9 "Make a boat with three decks and many rooms," God told Noah, "and cover it with a roof." It took Noah a long time to build such a huge boat, but he did exactly as God had commanded him.

10 "All kinds of birds and animals will be taken into the ark," God told Noah. God wanted to save a male and a female of every kind of animal from the coming destruction.

11 Noah and his wife and his three sons and their wives would have to live in the ark for a long time, so they put on board enough food for themselves and for the animals.

12 As soon as all the preparations were completed, Noah and his family entered the ark and God shut the door. Then, as God had said, rain began to fall. The destruction of the world had begun!

The Ark Comes to Rest

1 On the day the rain began to fall, Noah and his family entered the ark. It rained and rained for forty days and nights, but the ark floated on top of the water.

2 The water became so deep that it covered even the highest mountains. All the animals, all the birds, and all the people on the earth died in the flood. Only those with Noah in the ark remained alive.

3 But God had not forgotten Noah. He caused a wind to blow, and the wind began to make the water slowly go down.

4 After 150 days the ark finally stopped floating and came to rest on top of a mountain called Ararat. Noah and his family stayed in the ark and waited as the waters continued to go down.

5 Forty days later Noah opened the window of the ark and sent out a raven. It did not come back but just kept flying around and around until the water was completely gone.

6 Next Noah sent out a dove to check whether the water was gone. The dove could find no place to light and returned to the ark.

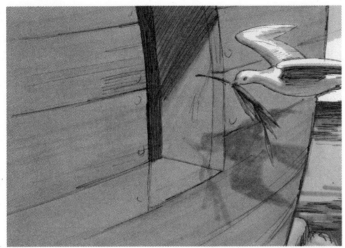

7 Seven days later Noah sent out the dove again. This time it returned to the ark with a freshly plucked olive leaf in its beak. Noah knew by this that the water had gone down below the tree tops.

8 Still another seven days passed before Noah sent the dove out again. This time it did not come back at all. Noah knew that it was now safe for him and his family to leave the ark.

9 Then God said, "Noah, it's time for you and your family to get off the ark and bring out all the birds and animals so that they can have babies and spread all over the earth."

10 When Noah got off the ark, he built an altar to the Lord. God was pleased with Noah's offering. God told Noah that it was all right to eat meat from then on, but that no one should kill another human being.

11 God blessed Noah and his family and said to them, "You must have many children so that your descendants will live all over the earth."

12 Then God made a promise never again to destroy all the living things on the earth with a flood. The rainbow would be a reminder of that promise. Thus was the old world destroyed and the new begun.

Abram Leaves His Home

1 Many years after God destroyed the world by flood, a man named Abram journeyed with his father and his family from their home in Ur to Haran. There Abram's father died. And there God spoke to Abram.

2 "Go from this country to a land that I will show you," God said. "I will give you many descendants and they will become a great nation, and through you I will bless all the peoples on earth."

3 So Abram did as God commanded. He left his home to go to the land of Canaan far away. Abram took with him his wife Sarai, his nephew Lot, and all his riches and slaves.

4 When Abram got to Canaan, he camped at a place called Shechem. There God appeared to Abram, saying, "This is the land I am going to give you and your children."

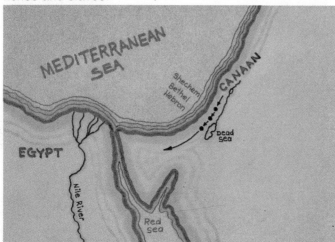

5 Abram built an altar to the Lord at that place. Then Abram moved on south. There was a bad famine in Canaan at that time, so Abram decided to go on down to Egypt for a while.

6 But Abram was worried. He was afraid the Egyptians would kill him in order to take Sarai, because she was so beautiful. So he told her to say that she was his sister, not his wife.

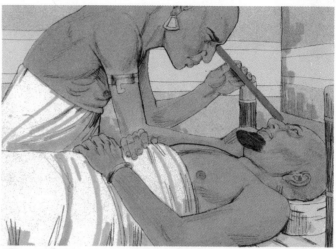

7 Just as Abram had feared, when they got to Egypt the king wanted Sarai for his wife. The king had her brought to his palace and he gave gifts to Abram.

8 But it was not right for the king to take another man's wife as his own, so God caused terrible diseases to strike the king and the other Egyptians living in the palace.

9 When the king figured out what had happened, he told Abram to take Sarai and go away. The king's men took Abram and his wife and sent them out of Egypt.

10 So Abram returned to Canaan. Soon his servants and Lot's servants began to have fights. Both men had large herds of sheep and goats, and there was not enough grass to feed them all.

11 "Quarreling and fighting are bad," Abram said to Lot. "Let's live in different places so there won't be any more trouble." Lot agreed and decided to move to Sodom. Abram stayed near Hebron.

12 Then the Lord spoke to Abram again. "This land will belong to your descendants forever," he said. "And I will give you so many descendants that you won't be able to count them all."

God's Covenant with Abraham

1 God had promised Abram many, many descendants. But Abram was now 85 years old and still had no children at all.

2 Finally he and his wife Sarai became discouraged. They decided to try to solve the problem themselves. Sarai gave her maid Hagar to Abram as his concubine, or second wife.

3 Hagar and Abram had a baby boy whom they named Ishmael. Abram thought that perhaps Ishmael was the child God promised.

4 But God said, "I will bless Sarai, who will now be called Sarah. She will be the mother of the son I promised you. From now on you will be called Abraham, for you will be the father of a great nation."

5 Then God said to Abraham, "You and your descendants must agree to circumcise every male among you. Every baby boy must be circumcised when he is eight days old."

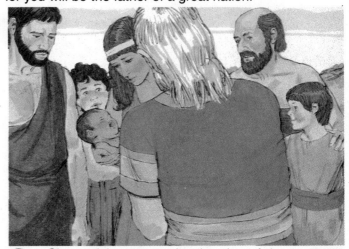

6 Circumcision was to be the sign of the covenant between God and the family of Abraham. So that very day Abraham and his son Ishmael and all his male slaves were circumcised.

7 One day, some time later, Abraham was sitting at the entrance to his tent during the hottest part of the day. Suddenly he looked up and saw three strangers standing nearby.

8 Abraham invited them to stop and eat with him. He provided water for washing their feet and food for their dinner. Abraham himself served the meal, while Sarah remained inside the tent.

9 During the meal, one of the men surprised Abraham by suddenly saying, "Nine months from now I will come back and your wife Sarah will have a son."

10 Sarah, listening from inside the tent, laughed to herself when she heard that. How could she possibly have a baby at her age?

11 But the man knew Sarah had laughed, thinking his promise ridiculous. "Is anything too hard for the Lord?" he asked. "Nine months from now I will return and Sarah will have a son, just as I have said."

12 When the meal was finished, Abraham walked a little way with the three visitors as they started their journey again, leaving Sarah to wonder about their strange promise.

God Tests Abraham

1 When Abraham was 100 years old, Sarah gave birth to a son. This was the child God had promised Abraham and Sarah for so long.

2 Abraham named the child Isaac. When Isaac was eight days old, Abraham circumcised him, just as God had commanded.

3 Time passed. Then one day the Lord tested Abraham. He told Abraham to take Isaac to a certain mountain and there to offer him as a sacrifice to God.

4 Early the next morning, Abraham cut wood for the sacrifice and loaded it on his donkey. He took Isaac and two servants and started out for the mountain which God had described.

5 On the third day they could see the mountain in the distance. Abraham said to the servants, "Stay here with the donkey. Isaac and I will go the mountain and worship. We will be back soon."

6 Abraham had Isaac carry the wood for the sacrifice, while he himself carried a knife and live coals for starting the fire.

7 On the way to the mountain, Isaac asked, "Father, where is the lamb for the sacrifice?" Abraham answered, "God himself will provide one."

8 When they came to the right place, Abraham built an altar and arranged the wood on it. Next he tied up Isaac, his dear son, and placed him upon the wood on the altar.

9 Just as Abraham raised the knife to kill his son, the angel of the Lord stopped him. The angel said, "Don't hurt the boy. Now I know that you honor God."

10 Abraham then noticed a ram whose horns were caught in a nearby bush. He offered this ram as a sacrifice in the place of his son Isaac.

11 Then God said, "I, the Lord, will richly bless you because you did not keep back even your only son from me."

12 "Your descendants will be as numerous as the stars in the sky, and through them all nations will be blessed—all because you obeyed my commands." Abraham's faith had passed God's test.

A Wife for Isaac

1 Sarah died when she was 127 years old. Abraham bought a piece of land with a cave on it so Sarah could be buried near where they lived in the land of Canaan.

2 Abraham was very old. Isaac was grown now, but he was not yet married. So Abraham ordered his servant to go back to the country where he had lived before to get a wife for Isaac from among his relatives.

3 Abraham told his servant not to take Isaac back there but to bring his wife-to-be to Canaan, the land the Lord had promised to give to Abraham's descendants.

4 So the servant took ten camels and went to the city where Abraham's brother lived. He stopped at a well outside the city where the women came in late afternoon to get water.

5 The servant prayed that the Lord would help him find the right woman to be Isaac's wife.

6 Before he had finished his prayer, a beautiful young girl came to the well carrying a water jar on her shoulder. She filled the jar at the well and started back home.

7 The servant ran to her and asked for a drink. She gave him water and said, "I will also water your camels." This was the very sign for which the servant had prayed!

8 After the girl watered the camels, the servant talked with her and found out that her name was Rebekah and that she was a relative of Abraham! Then the servant worshiped God for helping him find this girl.

9 Rebekah ran home and told her family what had happened. Her brother Laban then went to the well and invited Abraham's servant to come spend the night in his house.

10 Then the servant explained about Abraham. He told how Abraham wanted a wife for Isaac from among his relatives and how the Lord had led him to Rebekah.

11 Rebekah's father and brother gave their permission for Rebekah to go to be Isaac's wife. It was clear that this was what God wanted. So the servant and Rebekah set off for Canaan the next day.

12 Isaac took Rebekah to be his wife, and he loved her. Thus he was comforted by Rebekah after the death of his mother.

Jacob and Esau

■ Although Isaac and Rebekah had been married for a long time, they still had no children. So Isaac prayed for a child, and the Lord answered his prayer.

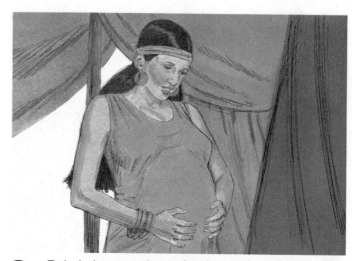

2 Rebekah was going to be the mother of twins! Before they were born, they struggled with each other inside her body. Rebekah prayed, asking the Lord what this meant.

The Lord said, "Two nations are within you; you will give birth to two rival peoples. One will be stronger than the other, and the older will serve the younger."

4 So Rebekah gave birth to twin boys. The first one was reddish and hairy. They named him Esau.

5 The second boy was born holding on tightly to the heel of his brother Esau. They named this one Jacob.

6 Time passed, and the boys grew up. Esau became a skilled hunter, a man who loved the outdoors. But Jacob was very different. He was a quiet man who stayed at home.

7 Esau was the favorite son of Isaac, who loved the meat that Esau brought home from his hunts. Jacob was his mother's favorite.

8 One day Esau came in from hunting just as Jacob was cooking some stew. Esau was very hungry and asked his brother for some of the stew.

9 Jacob said, "All right, I'll give it to you if you will give me your rights as the firstborn son."

10 In those days, when the father died the firstborn son got twice as much of the family wealth as the other sons. He became the head of the family. Thus the rights of the firstborn were very valuable.

11 But Esau said, "Well, I am about to starve to death, so what good will my rights be?" So he promised Jacob with an oath that he would turn over to Jacob his rights as firstborn son.

12 Esau ate the stew his brother gave him and went out. That was all he cared about his rights as first-born son. Later, Esau would be sorry he had done such a foolish thing!

Jacob Tricks His Brother

1 Isaac was now very old and blind. He decided that before he died he would give his final blessing to his firstborn son Esau.

2 Isaac asked Esau to kill some game so that he could prepare his father's favorite food. After Isaac ate the meal, he would give his final blessing.

3 Rebekah overheard this plan and told Jacob about it. Because Jacob was her favorite son, she wanted him to get the blessing. She ordered Jacob to bring her two goats.

4 Rebekah cooked the goat meat the way Isaac liked it and dressed Jacob in Esau's clothes. Esau was very hairy, so she tied goat skins on Jacob's arms and neck to fool Isaac in case he touched him.

5 When Jacob brought the meat to his father, Isaac was suspicious at first because the voice was not like Esau's. But when he touched the hairy skin, he thought it must be Esau after all.

6 After he ate the food Jacob brought, he had his son come close so that he could kiss him. Then he could smell Esau's clothes which Jacob wore.

7 So he blessed Jacob, thinking he was Esau. He prayed that God would make him wealthy and a powerful ruler over his brother and his relatives.

8 After Jacob left, Esau returned. When he asked his father for the blessing, Isaac realized he had blessed someone else. He began to tremble and shake.

9 Esau cried out bitterly and loudly and asked Isaac to bless him, too. But Isaac said, "Your brother has deceived me and taken away your blessing."

10 "There is nothing I can do for you, Son," Isaac said sadly. Isaac told Esau that Esau would be Jacob's slave for a time but that some day he would get free of Jacob's control.

11 After that, Esau hated Jacob. "This is the second time Jacob has cheated me. He took away my rights as firstborn son and now my blessing," Esau thought. He decided to kill Jacob.

12 But Rebekah found out what Esau planned to do. She asked Isaac to send Jacob to her brother Laban's home to find a wife, thinking Jacob could return home when Esau got over his anger.

Jacob's Trip to Haran

1 Esau, angry with Jacob for stealing his blessing, planned to kill him. So Isaac and Rebekah sent Jacob away to Haran. There he would be safe, and he could get a wife from among their relatives.

2 After his first day's journey, Jacob stopped to camp for the night. He lay down to sleep, using a stone as a pillow. And then he had a dream.

3 In his dream he saw a stairway reaching from earth to heaven, with angels going up and down on it. And there was the Lord, standing before him!

4 The Lord promised Jacob many descendants, as he had promised his father Isaac and his grandfather Abraham. God promised also to be with Jacob and bring him safely to the land of Canaan.

5 Then Jacob awoke and said, "The Lord is in this place, and I didn't know it. This place must be the house of God; it must be the gate that opens into heaven."

6 The next morning Jacob took the stone he had used as a pillow and set it up as a memorial. He poured oil on the stone to dedicate it to God. Jacob named the place Bethel, which means "House of God."

7 Then Jacob made a vow to God. "If you will be with me and protect me on this journey so that I return safely to my father's home, then you will be my God."

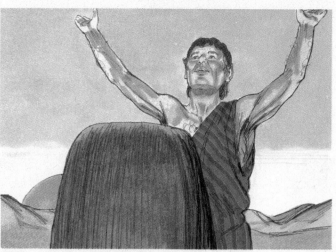

8 "This memorial stone which I have set up will be the place where you are worshiped, and I will give you a tenth of everything you give me."

9 Then Jacob started his trip again. One day he came to a well which was covered with a large stone. There were three flocks of sheep lying in the fields around the well.

10 When Jacob talked with the shepherds there, he found out that they were from Haran and knew his uncle Laban.

11 While Jacob was still talking to the shepherds, Laban's daughter Rachel arrived with his flock. Jacob moved away the stone from the well so that she could water her father's flocks.

12 He told her he was her relative, the son of Rebekah. She ran to tell her father, who welcomed his nephew into his home. Jacob stayed there quite a while.

Jacob Gets Two Wives

1 Because of Esau's anger, Jacob had been sent to Haran, where he lived with his uncle, Laban.

2 Laban had two daughters. Rachel, the younger daughter, was more beautiful than Leah, the older one. Jacob soon fell in love with Rachel.

3 Laban offered to pay Jacob to work for him, but Jacob said, "I will work seven years for you if you will let me marry Rachel."

4 Laban agreed, so Jacob worked for him for a full seven years. But the time seemed like only a few days to him because of his love for Rachel.

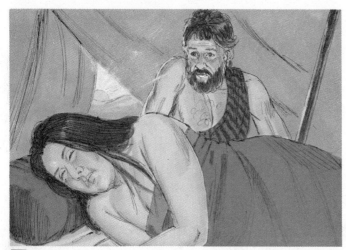

5 When seven years had passed, Laban gave a wedding feast for Jacob. But that night he sent Leah instead of Rachel to Jacob. The next morning Jacob awoke to discover that Laban had tricked him.

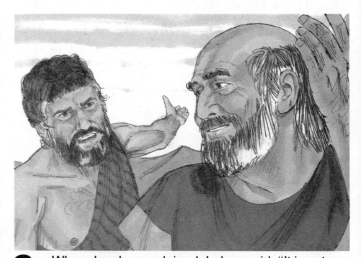

6 When Jacob complained, Laban said, "It is not our custom to let the younger daughter marry before the older. But I will give you Rachel now if you will work for me for another seven years."

7 Jacob agreed to that. When the week of marriage celebrations was over, Laban gave Jacob his other daughter Rachel to be his wife, too. Jacob loved Rachel more than Leah.

8 While Jacob lived in Haran, he became the father of many children. His two wives and their two slave girls, Bilhah and Zilpah, bore him eleven sons. The son of Rachel, Jacob's favorite, was Joseph.

9 After his son Joseph was born, Jacob wanted to return home to Canaan. Laban, however, knew that God had blessed him because of Jacob, so he asked Jacob to stay longer.

10 Jacob agreed to stay longer if Laban would give him all the black lambs and all the spotted or speckled goats. This would make it easy to know which animals belonged to Laban and which belonged to Jacob.

11 In a dream, God told Jacob how to increase his flocks of sheep and herds of goats. Gradually Jacob became very wealthy and his flocks became much larger than Laban's. Laban grew angry with Jacob.

12 God was now ready for Jacob to return to his home in Canaan, the land of his fathers. Jacob's departure was to lead to trouble between Jacob and his uncle Laban.

Jacob Returns to Canaan

1 After many years of working for his uncle Laban, Jacob wanted to take his wives and children and go back home to Canaan.

2 Jacob was afraid his uncle would try to stop him, so he did not let Laban know he was leaving. While Laban was gone to shear his sheep, Jacob packed up his possessions and left with his family in a hurry.

3 Three days later, Laban found out that Jacob had left. Laban took his men and chased Jacob for seven days. But God warned Laban in a dream not to threaten Jacob in any way.

4 When Laban saw Jacob, he said, "Why did you run off without telling me? I would have given you a celebration. I didn't even have a chance to say goodbye to my daughters and grandchildren."

5 Then Laban accused Jacob of stealing his household gods. Jacob said that he had not taken them and that he would put to death anyone who had. He did not know that his own wife Rachel had stolen them.

6 Laban searched through all the tents. When he went through Rachel's tent, she said she could not get up because she was feeling sick. But Rachel had hidden the stolen gods under the camel saddle she lay on.

7 When Laban could not find the stolen gods, Jacob became angry. He had worked long and hard for Laban and now Laban had accused him of stealing.

8 But they decided that they would make a promise not to fight each other. Jacob and Laban made a pile of stones to remind them of their agreement.

9 The next morning Laban kissed his daughters and grandchildren goodbye and left to go back home. Jacob also continued his trip home to Canaan.

10 Jacob was worried about how his brother Esau might feel about him, so he sent messengers to greet Esau and to ask for his favor.

11 The messengers came back and reported, "Esau is already on the way to meet you. He has 400 men with him!"

12 Jacob was frightened, thinking that Esau might be planning to attack him. So Jacob placed all the animals and all the people with him in two groups. If Esau attacked one group, the other could escape.

Jacob Meets Esau Again

1 Jacob learned that Esau was coming to meet him with 400 men. Fearing that Esau might be planning to attack him, Jacob prepared for the worst.

2 Jacob prayed, reminding God of his promise to give him more descendants than anyone could count. "Save me from my brother Esau. I'm afraid he is coming to destroy us all—even the women and children."

3 The next day Jacob got together a big present for Esau: 220 goats, 220 sheep, thirty camels, fifty cattle, and thirty donkeys. He grouped them in herds and sent them ahead, one group at a time.

4 He instructed his servants to say, "Jacob sends these animals as a gift to his master Esau. Jacob himself is right behind us." Jacob thought these gifts might make his brother forgive him.

5 That night Jacob sent his herds and his family ahead. Alone, Jacob had a strange experience—someone came and wrestled with him all night. The stranger blessed Jacob and gave him the name "Israel."

6 The next day Jacob caught up with his family. When he could see Esau coming with 400 men, he divided his family and put Rachel and Joseph in the back where they would be safest.

7 Then Jacob went ahead of them and bowed seven times before Esau. But Esau ran up to Jacob and threw his arms around Jacob and kissed him. Both of them were crying.

8 Esau tried to refuse the gifts of animals Jacob had given him. But Jacob said, "Please accept my gift. To see your face is for me like seeing the face of God, now that you have been so friendly to me."

9 Jacob told Esau to go on home and that he would come along later. His herds and his children were weak and tired from the long journey, so he wanted time for them to rest.

10 According to instructions of the Lord, Jacob stopped at Bethel, where he had once seen the stairway to heaven in a dream. There he built an altar to the Lord.

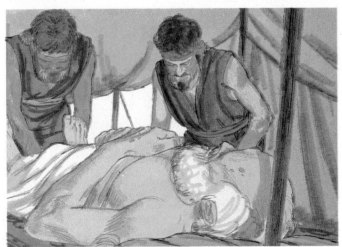

11 As Jacob and his family traveled, Rachel gave birth to a second son, Benjamin. But Rachel died when the baby was born. Jacob buried her there, near the road going to Bethlehem.

12 Finally Jacob reached Hebron, where his father Isaac was living. Isaac died later when he was 180 years old. He was buried by his sons, Esau and Jacob. Now the story of Jacob's son Joseph begins.

Joseph's Dreams Cause Trouble

1 Joseph was the son of Rachel, the wife whom Jacob had loved most. Joseph's mother had died giving birth to Benjamin as the family returned to Canaan from Haran.

2 Jacob loved Joseph more than all his other sons. He made a long coat with full sleeves for Joseph. Joseph's brothers were very jealous of Joseph and would not even speak to him in a friendly way.

3 Joseph was now seventeen years old. He helped his brothers take care of his father's sheep and goats. But he brought bad reports to his father about what his brothers were doing.

4 One day Joseph had a dream, which he explained to his brothers. "We were all in the field tying up sheaves of wheat. My sheaf stood up and yours made a circle around mine and bowed down to it," he said.

5 This made his brothers very angry. "Do you think you are going to be a king and rule over us?" they asked. So they hated him even more when they heard about his dream.

6 Then Joseph had another dream, which he also told to his brothers. He said, "I saw the sun, the moon, and the eleven stars bowing down to me."

7 Joseph told his father Jacob about this dream, too. His father scolded him, saying, "Do you think that your mother and brothers and I are going to bow down to you?"

8 But his father kept thinking about the things Joseph had dreamed.

9 One day Joseph's brothers had gone to Shechem to take care of their father's flock.

10 Jacob called Joseph and told him to go to Shechem to see whether his brothers and the flock were all right and then come back and tell him.

11 Joseph went to Shechem and wandered around the country looking for his brothers. He found a young man who told him that his brothers had already left there and gone on to a place called Dothan.

12 So Joseph headed for Dothan to catch up with his brothers and the flock. Little did he know what a terrible experience he was about to have!

Joseph Is Sold

1 As Joseph traveled toward Dothan to find his brothers, they were tending their flocks in the nearby hills.

2 Suddenly the brothers saw Joseph coming in the distance. They remembered his boastful dreams and how they hated him because of the dreams.

3 "Here comes that dreamer!" said one of the brothers. "Now's our chance—let's kill him!"

4 Reuben knew the brothers were too angry to be reasonable. But he didn't want to be guilty of killing Joseph. "Let's just put him down that dry well," he said.

5 The brothers agreed to Reuben's plan. They did not know that Reuben was secretly planning to come back later and rescue Joseph.

6 When Joseph entered their camp, the brothers jumped on him. They roughly stripped off his brightly colored coat and threw him down the nearby dry well.

7 Later, while Reuben was taking his turn watching the herds, the other brothers sat down to supper. Joseph was still deep in the well, pleading with them to set him free.

8 While they were eating, the brothers saw a caravan of traders passing nearby. "Let's sell Joseph to these slavers. We can be rid of him and make some money, too!" So Joseph was sold to the traders.

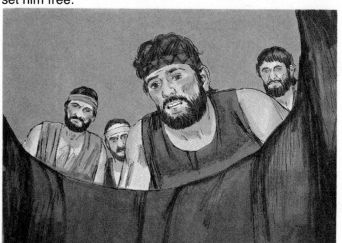

9 When Reuben returned hours later and discovered that the well was empty, he cried in great sadness, "Joseph is gone! How shall we face our father?"

10 To cover up their crime, the brothers tore Joseph's coat, dipped it in goat's blood, and took it to their father. "We found this in the field," they lied.

11 "A wild beast has eaten him!" Jacob cried, as he tore his clothes in sorrow. Jacob was so full of grief for Joseph that he could hardly stand to live.

12 Meanwhile, while Jacob grieved in Canaan, Joseph was carried far away to Egypt and sold as a slave.

Joseph in Egypt

1 After his brothers sold him to slave traders, Joseph was taken to Egypt. There his situation got even worse.

2 When the slavers arrived in Egypt, they sold Joseph to Potiphar, who was captain of the bodyguard of the king, or Pharaoh.

3 God gave Joseph a special talent for organizing his work well. Because of God's blessing, everything Joseph tried to do, he did well.

4 Potiphar was so impressed with this young slave's abilities that after a while he made Joseph manager over his entire household. Joseph was even in charge of much of Potiphar's business!

5 Joseph was young, strong, talented, and good-looking. But trouble would not stay away!

6 About this time, Potiphar's wife began to notice what a fine young man Joseph was. She began to pay lots of attention to him.

7 Joseph knew her flirting was not right. He tried to avoid her and to have nothing to do with her.

8 But one day while Potiphar was away, his wife grabbed Joseph by his clothing. "Come with me," she said.

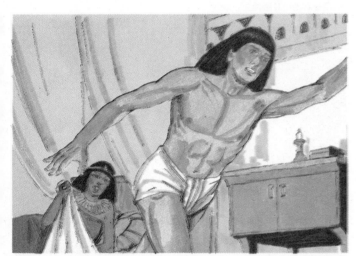

9 Joseph did not know a good way to get out of this situation. So he quickly slipped out of his garment and ran from the house.

10 Potiphar's wife was left holding Joseph's empty garment. She screamed in rage. Others in the household came running. "Joseph attacked me!" Potiphar's wife cried.

11 That evening when Potiphar came home, his wife repeated the lie, using the other servants as witnesses. "Joseph attacked me! When I screamed, he ran away. See, here is his garment!"

12 Potiphar was so angry that he threw Joseph into prison. But even here God blessed Joseph. Because of his talents and his good behavior, he soon was put in charge of the entire prison.

Joseph in Prison

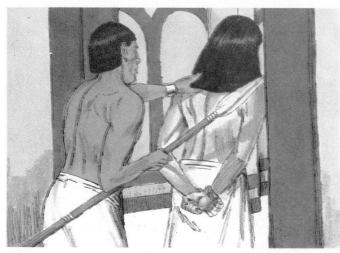

1 Joseph was imprisoned unfairly, but God was with him still. Even in prison Joseph was successful in what he did.

2 Some time later, Pharaoh became angry with two of his servants—his chief baker and his butler. He had them thrown into prison. Joseph met them and became their friend.

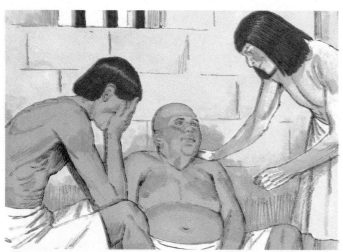

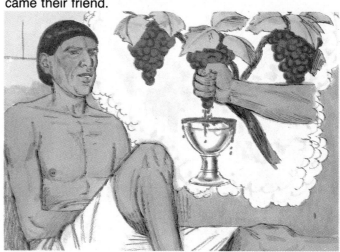

3 One night, both of these men had disturbing dreams. The next morning, Joseph noticed their unhappy faces and said, "Tell me your dreams."

4 The butler spoke first. "In my dream I saw a vine with three branches. It budded and filled with grapes. I squeezed them into Pharaoh's cup and gave him a drink."

5 Joseph smiled. "Your dream has a happy meaning. Three days from now, Pharaoh is going to take you out of prison and give your job back to you."

6 Joseph continued, "When this happens, please try to help me if you can. I am a foreigner—a Hebrew. As a youth I was kidnapped and sold into slavery. I am now in prison for a crime I did not do."

7 The butler promised that he would help. Then Joseph listened to the baker's dream. "I dreamed I was carrying three baskets of baked goods on my head," began the baker.

8 "But before I could deliver them to Pharaoh, a great cloud of birds came and ate all the loaves and cakes."

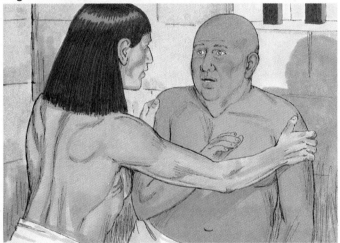

9 Joseph's face was saddened. "My friend, prepare yourself for bad news! Your dream means that three days from now you will be put to death by Pharaoh's order."

10 Sure enough, Pharaoh's birthday came three days later. He gave a party for all the people who worked in his government and on his staff.

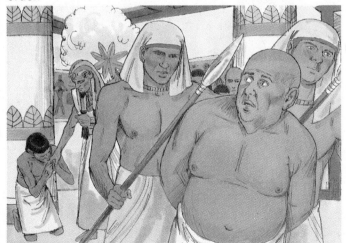

11 Just as Joseph had predicted, the butler was restored to Pharaoh's service, but the chief baker was sentenced to die a terrible death.

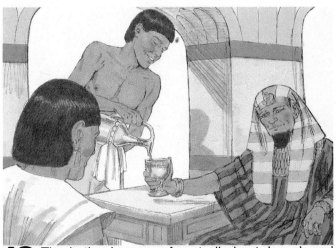

12 The butler, however, forgot all about Joseph and his promise to help him.

Pharaoh's Dream

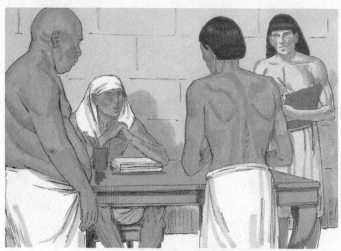

1 While Joseph was still in prison in Egypt, something happened which changed his life and the future of all Egypt.

2 One night Pharaoh had a very disturbing dream. The next morning he became very worried about what the dream might mean.

3 Pharaoh called together the wisest magicians and thinkers of Egypt and told them about his dream, but they were just as confused about it as he was.

4 Then Pharaoh's butler spoke up. "Now I remember—back when the baker and I were in jail, we both had strange dreams. A young Hebrew explained them and everything came true as he said!"

5 "Find this man immediately!" cried Pharaoh. So Joseph was taken from the prison and brought before Pharaoh.

6 Pharaoh told Joseph his dream: "Out of the Nile River came seven fat cows, followed soon after by seven thin cows. Then the thin cows ate the fat cows!"

7 "Soon afterward I had another dream. Seven plump ears of grain sprouted from a stalk, followed by seven withered ears. The withered ears ate up the plump ears!"

8 "God is trying to tell you the same thing in both dreams," explained Joseph. "The seven fat cows and plump ears mean that Egypt is going to have seven years of good crops and great wealth."

9 "But these years of plenty will be followed by seven years of famine, when crops will be poor and no one will have enough food," continued Joseph. "That's what the thin cows and withered ears mean."

10 "The famine will be so terrible that it will make everyone forget the seven good years. God has planned all this, and it is going to happen soon."

11 Seeing Pharaoh's dismay, Joseph added, "I would suggest that Pharaoh find a wise man to help the country prepare for this emergency."

12 Pharaoh said to his assistants, "Who could be better than Joseph? The Spirit of God is clearly in him." Then he proclaimed, "I appoint Joseph Prime Minister of Egypt. Only I will outrank him."

Joseph Rules Egypt

1 Just as Joseph had said, Egypt had seven years of plentiful crops. Joseph collected a portion of all the grain grown in Egypt and stored it. Then a great famine struck the land.

2 In Canaan, Jacob said to his sons, "I have heard that there is grain in Egypt. Go down and buy some for us before we all starve to death!"

3 All the sons left for Egypt except Benjamin, the youngest. Jacob was afraid something might happen to him as it had to Joseph years ago.

4 Since Joseph was Prime Minister of Egypt and in charge of grain sales, his brothers came before him, not knowing who he was, and bowed low. (Remember Joseph's boyhood dreams?)

5 Joseph recognized them instantly, but they did not know him. Joseph decided to test his brothers. "You are spies!" he charged.

6 "Sir," they responded, "we are not spies. We are all brothers, and our father is in Canaan. Our youngest brother is there, and one of our brothers is dead."

7 Joseph knew they spoke the truth. But he wanted to test his brothers and make his authority clear to them, so he had them all thrown into jail.

8 After three days, Joseph said, "All of you, except one, may go. That one will be held here until you return with your youngest brother. Then I will know you have told the truth."

9 The brothers cried to each other in their own language, "All of this has happened to us because of the terrible thing we did to Joseph long ago. We heard his pleading but would not listen!"

10 Joseph, of course, understood their words and was so touched by the brothers' repentance that he had to slip into a nearby room where he could hide his tears.

11 Then Joseph selected Simeon as the brother who would have to stay in Egypt. He ordered his servants to fill the other brothers' sacks with grain.

12 But Joseph also gave secret instructions to put each brother's payment at the top of his sack.

Trouble in Egypt

1 Joseph's brothers started home to Canaan with the grain they bought in Egypt. But when they stopped for the night, one of them discovered his money in the top of his sack. They were confused and afraid.

2 Back at home, they told their father Jacob about all that had happened to them. Then when they opened their sacks, every one of them found his money in his sack! This really frightened them.

3 Jacob was very troubled. He had now lost two sons, and he didn't want anything to happen to Benjamin. But the famine in Canaan got worse and finally all the grain they had bought was used up.

4 When Jacob told his sons to go back to Egypt and buy more food, they explained that they had to take Benjamin with them. Finally Jacob unhappily agreed for them to take Benjamin.

5 When the brothers got back to Egypt, they tried to return the money they had found in their sacks. But Joseph's servant refused, saying, "I have already been paid." Then he sent out their brother Simeon.

6 Joseph invited the brothers to eat dinner with him at noon. When he saw Benjamin, he was so happy he felt like crying. He went to another room until he was through crying.

7 Then the feast was served. When the brothers saw they were seated in order of age from oldest to youngest, they were amazed. They were also surprised by the extra large servings of food given Benjamin.

8 Joseph secretly told his servant to fill the brothers' sacks with grain and to put each man's money in the top of his sack. Joseph also told the servant to put his special silver cup in Benjamin's sack.

9 Early the next day the brothers started for home. Then Joseph ordered his servant to chase them and say, "Why have you stolen my master's silver cup? You've done a very wicked thing."

10 The brothers exclaimed, "We have stolen nothing!" They swore that if the cup were found with any one of them they would all be slaves. The servant searched and found the cup in Benjamin's sack!

11 The shocked brothers tore their clothes in sorrow and returned to Joseph, who said, "Didn't you know I would find out?" Judah asked, "How can we prove our innocence? Now we are all your slaves."

12 But Joseph said, "Only Benjamin, in whose sack the cup was found, will become a slave. The rest of you are free to go home." The brothers knew that they could not face their father without Benjamin.

"I Am Joseph"

1 Thinking they would be made slaves for stealing the Egyptian Prime Minister's silver cup, the sons of Jacob were surprised when they were told that all but Benjamin were free to return home.

2 But Judah said to the Prime Minister, "Sir, if I go back without Benjamin, my father will die. I cannot face him without Benjamin. Let me stay here in his place and send him home with my other brothers."

3 At this point Joseph could no longer control his feelings, so he sent everyone out of the room except his brothers. He cried with such loud sobs that even the Egyptians outside could hear him.

4 Then he said to the sons of Jacob, "I am Joseph, your brother." When they heard this they were so terrified that they could not answer.

5 Then Joseph said, "Do not be upset or blame yourselves because you sold me here. It was really God who sent me here ahead of you to save your lives."

6 "There will be five more years of famine, so go get our father and bring him here and live in the land of Goshen. Then I can take care of you during the famine so that you will not starve."

7 Then Joseph threw his arms around Benjamin and began to cry. Benjamin also cried as he hugged his brother. Still weeping, Joseph hugged each of his other brothers and kissed them.

8 The Pharaoh was pleased to learn that Joseph's brothers had come to Egypt. He invited them to bring their father and live there. So Joseph sent them home with gifts and food to get their father Jacob.

9 As soon as they got back home, they told Jacob that Joseph was alive and was the ruler of all Egypt. Jacob was so surprised that he couldn't believe it at first. But finally he said, "I must go see Joseph."

10 So Jacob loaded up all his possessions and his livestock and took his whole family to Egypt. The total number of descendants he took with him was 66, not counting his sons' wives.

11 When Jacob arrived in Goshen, Joseph climbed into a chariot and went to meet him. Seeing his father for the first time after so many years, Joseph threw his arms around Jacob's neck and wept.

12 After living in Egypt seventeen years, Jacob died. Joseph took Jacob's body back to Canaan to bury him beside his father Isaac and grandfather Abraham in the land God had promised him.

The Israelites Become Slaves

1 A long time had passed since the family of Jacob moved to Egypt. Joseph and his brothers and all the people living then were now dead. But their descendants had become very numerous.

2 Then a new king, or Pharaoh, came to power in Egypt. He did not remember Joseph or the promises that had been made to Joseph's family to treat them well. This Pharaoh feared the Israelites.

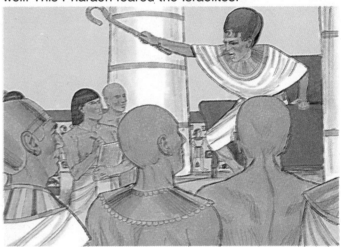

3 Pharaoh thought, "Now that there are so many Israelites, they might be dangerous to Egypt! If any enemy attacks, the Israelites might help them and then escape from Egypt."

4 So Pharaoh made a plan to keep the Israelites from growing in numbers. He decided he would make slaves of the Israelites and crush their spirits with hard labor.

5 The Egyptians made the Israelites work as slaves in the fields and build cities of brick and mortar. They built the cities of Pithom and Rameses, which were great supply centers.

6 But the more the Egyptians oppressed the Israelites, the more the Israelites increased in number and the farther they spread through the land.

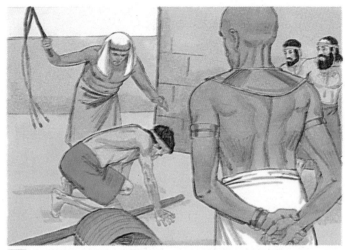

7 Now all the Egyptians began to be afraid of the Israelites. So they made the lives of the Israelites miserable with hard labor.

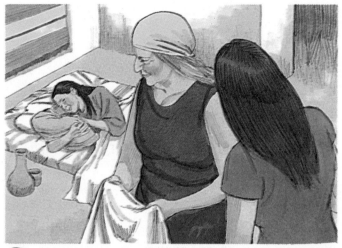

8 There were two Hebrew women who worked as midwives, helping the other Hebrew women when their babies were born. Their names were Shiphrah and Puah.

9 The Pharaoh gave orders to Shiphrah and Puah to kill all the baby boys who were born to Hebrew (or Israelite) women. But the midwives ignored Pharaoh's orders because they feared God.

10 When Pharaoh learned they were not obeying his orders, he called them to him. They gave him an excuse, saying, "The Hebrew women are so strong that they have their babies before we can arrive."

11 God was pleased with the midwives for not obeying Pharaoh's orders to kill the babies, and he blessed them with families of their own. The Israelites continued to grow in numbers.

12 Pharaoh, now angry, ordered all the Egyptian people to throw every newborn Hebrew boy into the Nile River. This is where the story of Moses, the man God sent to rescue the Israelites, begins.

The Birth of Moses

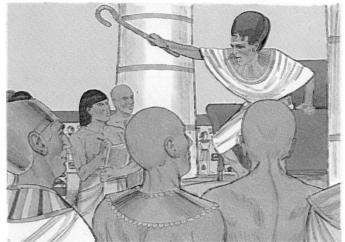

1 The Pharaoh of Egypt feared the Israelites because there were so many of them. So he made them work as slaves. Then he ordered that all baby boys born to the Israelites be thrown into the Nile River.

2 An Israelite of the tribe of Levi named Amram was at that time married to a woman named Jochebed, who was also of the tribe of Levi. During this time, Jochebed gave birth to a son.

3 His mother loved her baby boy, and of course she did not want him to be thrown into the Nile River. So she hid him in her house for three months.

4 Finally, hiding him became too dangerous. Jochebed made a basket of reeds and covered it with tar to make it waterproof.

5 When the little boat was finished, she placed her baby in it and hid it in the tall grass at the edge of the river. The baby's sister, Miriam, watched the basket from a distance to see what would happen.

6 Before long, Pharaoh's daughter came to the river to bathe. Her servants walked along the bank. Suddenly Pharaoh's daughter noticed the basket in the tall grass and sent a slave girl to get it.

7 When she opened the reed basket, she found the baby boy. He was crying and she felt sorry for him. She could tell that it was a Hebrew baby.

8 Then Miriam, who had been watching all this, came up to the Pharaoh's daughter. She asked the princess, "Would you like for me to get a Hebrew woman to nurse the baby?"

9 The princess said yes, so Miriam ran and brought her mother. The princess told Jochebed she would pay her to nurse the baby, so Jochebed was able to keep her baby in her own home without any danger.

10 When the boy was old enough, his mother took him to the home of Pharaoh's daughter.

11 The princess adopted the boy and named him "Moses," because she had pulled him out of the water. "Moses" sounds like the Hebrew word which means "pull out."

12 So Moses grew up in Pharaoh's household in Egypt. What he learned there would be very useful to him one day, because God intended for Moses to become the leader of the people of Israel.

Moses Flees to Midian

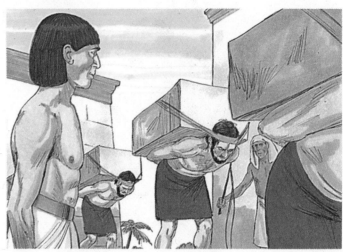

1 Pharaoh's daughter had found a Hebrew baby floating in a basket in the Nile River. She named the baby Moses and adopted him as her own son. Thus Moses grew up in the house of the Pharaoh!

2 But Moses never forgot that he was really a Hebrew and not an Egyptian. When he grew up, he went out to visit his people and saw the hard work they were forced to do for the Egyptians.

3 One day Moses saw an Egyptian beat a Hebrew, one of his own people.

4 Moses looked all around. When he saw that no one was looking, he killed the Egyptian and hid the body in the sand.

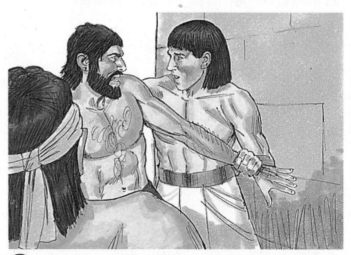

5 The next day Moses went back to the area where the Hebrews were living. This time he saw two Hebrews fighting with each other. He tried to stop the fight.

6 But the one who started the fight said to Moses, "Who made you our judge? Are you going to kill me as you killed that Egyptian?" Moses was afraid, because people had found out what he had done.

7 The news about Moses killing an Egyptian soon reached Pharaoh. He was very angry and ordered his men to kill Moses. However, Moses escaped and fled to the land of Midian.

8 One day Moses was sitting by a well. Seven girls, who were daughters of a priest of Midian named Jethro, came to the well to get water for their father's sheep and goats.

9 However, as the girls tried to get to the well, some shepherds drove them away. When Moses saw what was happening, he went to the aid of Jethro's daughters. He watered their animals for them.

10 Jethro was surprised when his daughters came home so early. They told him how an Egyptian had rescued them from the shepherds and watered their flocks.

11 Jethro sent his daughters back to invite Moses to his house. After talking with Jethro, Moses decided to live in Midian. He married Jethro's daughter Zipporah and had two sons, Gershom and Eliezer.

12 Years passed. The Pharaoh died, but the next Pharaoh still treated the Hebrews as slaves. They cried out to God. God heard them and remembered his covenant with Abraham, Isaac, and Jacob.

Moses and the Burning Bush

1 When the time was right, God prepared to deliver his people, the Hebrews, from their slavery in Egypt.

2 In Midian, Moses was taking care of the flock of his father-in-law Jethro. One day Moses led the flock across the desert to a holy mountain called Sinai.

3 There Moses suddenly noticed a bush that was on fire but did not seem to burn up. He was puzzled and went to take a closer look at it.

4 Then the Lord spoke to Moses from the midst of the burning bush. "Moses, Moses," the voice said. Moses answered, "Here I am."

5 Then the voice said, "Moses, take off your sandals, for you are in a holy place. I am the God of your ancestors, Abraham, Isaac, and Jacob." Moses hid his face, for he was afraid to look at God.

6 "I know about the sufferings of my people in Egypt. I have come down to rescue them and bring them out of Egypt to the land of Canaan."

7 "I am sending you to the Pharaoh so that you can lead my people out of his country," God said. "But I am nobody special," Moses said. "How can I bring the Israelites out of Egypt?"

8 "I will be with you. When you bring the people out of Egypt, you will worship me on this mountain. That will be the proof that I have sent you."

9 Then Moses said, "When I tell the Israelites, 'The God of your ancestors sent me to you,' they will say, 'What is his name?' So what shall I tell them?"

10 God said, "I am who I am. Tell them, 'The One who is called I AM has sent me to you.' This is my name forever; this is what all future generations are to call me."

11 "Explain to the leaders of Israel that I, the Lord, have decided to bring them out of Egypt. Then go with them to the Pharaoh and say, 'Let us go into the desert to worship the Lord our God.'"

12 Moses still was not sure he could do what God asked. But God showed him some miracles he could perform in Egypt. Then God told Moses that he could take his brother Aaron to help him.

Moses Confronts Pharaoh

1 At the burning bush, God assured Moses that he would be able to bring the Israelites out of Egypt. Moses went back to Midian, got his wife and sons, and set out for Egypt.

2 In the meantime God had appeared to Aaron, Moses' brother, and told him to go into the desert to meet Moses. When Aaron found Moses, he learned about God's plan.

3 So Moses and Aaron went back to Egypt. They told the leaders of the Israelites about God's plan. When the leaders saw the miracles, they believed that God was about to rescue them and they worshiped him.

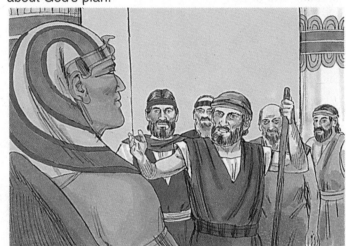

4 Moses and Aaron and the leaders of Israel went to the Pharaoh. They boldly said to him, "The Lord our God says, 'Let my people go, so that they can worship me in the desert.'"

5 But Pharaoh said, "Who is the Lord? Why should I listen to him and let you go?" Pharaoh was angry with them for causing the Hebrew slaves to do less work than before.

6 That same day Pharaoh commanded the Egyptian slave masters to stop giving the Hebrews straw. From now on they would have to find their own straw. But they had to make just as many bricks.

7 So the Hebrews had to go all over Egypt looking for straw. It took so much time that they couldn't make as many bricks as before. So the Egyptian slave masters beat the Hebrew foremen.

8 The foremen complained to Pharaoh, but he only told them to get back to work. Then they were angry with Moses and Aaron. "God will surely punish you for making Pharaoh hate us more," they said.

9 Moses himself was very upset that God had done nothing to help. What good had it done for God to send him if it had only made the Pharaoh treat the people worse?

10 God answered Moses, saying, "You are about to see what I will do to Pharaoh. I will force him to let my people go."

11 Moses told the people what God had said, but they would not believe him. Their cruel slavery had made them too discouraged.

12 The Lord told Moses to go before Pharaoh again and tell him to let the Israelites leave Egypt. God was now ready to use his power against Pharaoh.

God Reveals His Power

1 The Egyptian Pharaoh refused the Israelites permission to leave Egypt and made the lives of the Israelites even more miserable than before. So God told Moses to talk to Pharaoh again.

2 When Pharaoh demanded proof that what Moses and Aaron said was true, Aaron threw down his staff in front of Pharaoh and his officers. The staff changed into a snake!

3 Pharaoh called in his magicians, who were able to make their sticks turn into snakes, too. But then Aaron's staff swallowed up the other snakes! Yet Pharaoh stubbornly refused to listen to Moses.

4 Then the Lord told Moses and Aaron to meet Pharaoh at the Nile in the morning. "You have refused to let the Israelites go," Moses said, "so now you will find out who the Lord is by what he is going to do."

5 Aaron raised his staff and struck the river. All the water turned into blood! The fish in the river died and the smell was so bad that the people could not drink water from the river.

6 But again Pharaoh's magicians used their magic and were able to do the same thing. So Pharaoh refused to listen to Moses and went back to his palace.

7 Seven days passed. The Lord told Moses to go to Pharaoh again and tell him to let the people go. When Pharaoh refused, Aaron held his staff over the river. When he did, frogs came up out of it!

8 There were so many frogs that they covered the land. They came into the palace and into the homes of all the people. Frogs were in the beds and in the ovens and baking pans in the kitchens.

9 Pharaoh told Moses and Aaron to ask the Lord to take away the frogs. He promised that when the frogs were gone, he would let the Israelites go.

10 So Moses prayed and the frogs died. The Egyptians piled them up in great heaps and the land stank because of them. Then Pharaoh changed his mind and would not let the Israelites go.

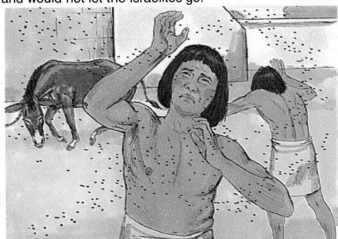

11 Next God told Moses to tell Aaron to strike the ground with his staff. That made the dust all over Egypt turn into gnats. They covered all the people and all the animals in Egypt.

12 The magicians tried to make gnats appear, but they couldn't. "God has done this!" they told Pharaoh. However, Pharaoh was still stubborn and refused to listen to Moses.

The Plagues Continue

1 Despite the first three plagues—blood, frogs, and gnats—the Pharaoh refused to let the Israelites go into the desert to worship God.

2 Therefore, the Lord sent great swarms of flies into Pharaoh's palace and the houses of his officials. But the flies did not enter Goshen, where the people of Israel lived.

3 Then Pharaoh told Moses to have the people offer their sacrifices in Egypt. But Moses said, "We cannot do that. If the Egyptians see us offer sacrifices, they will be offended and they will kill us."

4 Pharaoh then said they could go into the desert if they would not go too far. But when Moses prayed and the flies disappeared, Pharaoh became stubborn and would not let the people go.

5 So the Lord sent a terrible disease on all the animals. The Egyptians' horses, donkeys, camels, and cattle died. The animals of the Israelites, however, were not harmed. But still Pharaoh was stubborn.

6 Next the Lord told Moses to throw ashes into the air. All through the land the people and animals got terrible boils which became open sores. But Pharaoh would not obey the command of the Lord.

7 Then the Lord sent thunder and hail and lightning. It was the worst storm in Egypt's history. It killed all the people and animals out in the open and ruined the plants and trees.

8 There was no hail at all in the region of Goshen, where the Israelites lived. At Pharaoh's request, Moses prayed for the hail to stop. But again Pharaoh would not let the Israelites leave.

9 So the Lord sent Moses to warn Pharaoh about a locust plague. When the officials heard this, they were afraid. They urged Pharaoh to let the Israelites go.

10 Pharaoh told Moses and Aaron that the Israelites could go worship their God. But he would not let the women and children go. Then he drove Moses and Aaron out of his presence.

11 The Lord caused an east wind to blow in great swarms of locusts. They covered the ground until it was black. They ate everything the hail had not destroyed. Not a green thing was left in all of Egypt!

12 Then Pharaoh hurriedly called Moses and Aaron and admitted he had sinned against God. Moses prayed and God caused the wind to blow the locusts into the sea. But again Pharaoh changed his mind.

The Passover

1 In spite of the many plagues sent by God, the Pharaoh still refused to let the Israelites go into the desert to worship. Several times Pharaoh had said they could leave, only to change his mind.

2 So the Lord told Moses to raise his hand toward the sky. There was total darkness throughout Egypt for three days. The Egyptians could not see each other, and no one left his house during that time.

3 In the area where the Israelites lived, however, there was light. Pharaoh called Moses and said, "You may go worship the Lord. Your women and children may go, too. But all your animals must stay here."

4 Moses answered, "No, we must take our animals with us. We must select the animals with which to worship the Lord. But until we get there, we won't know what animals we are supposed to offer in sacrifice."

5 Pharaoh was very angry. "Get out of my sight! Don't let me ever see you here again! On the day I do, you will die!" Moses left him saying, "All right. You will not see me again."

6 The Lord said to Moses, "I will send only one more punishment on Egypt. After that, the Pharaoh will let you leave."

7 Moses delivered God's final message. "At midnight I will go through Egypt, and every firstborn son will die. Then you will know that I, the Lord, make a distinction between my people and the Egyptians."

8 Moses continued, "All your officials will come to me and bow down and beg me to take my people and go away. After that I will leave." Then in great anger Moses left the still stubborn Pharaoh.

9 Moses and the people prepared for their escape according to the Lord's instructions. They made ready for a celebration called the "Passover." First each family killed a young lamb or goat.

10 Then the fathers took some of the blood of the goat or lamb and smeared it on the doorposts and the beams above the doors of their houses, just as the Lord told them to do.

11 That night each family roasted its lamb or goat and ate it, along with bitter herbs and bread made without using yeast. Each person dressed for travel, ready to leave Egypt.

12 God told the Israelites to repeat the Passover celebration every year to remind them of this special night—the night God "passed over" their houses when he killed the firstborn sons of the Egyptians.

The Israelites Leave Egypt

1 In accordance with God's directions, the Israelites had smeared blood on their doorposts. That evening they celebrated the Passover feast in their homes. They were ready to leave Egypt.

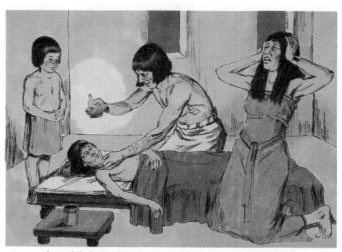

2 At midnight the Lord passed through the land and killed the firstborn son of every Egyptian family. Pharaoh and his officials were awakened by loud crying.

3 There was not one home in Egypt in which a son had not died. But the Lord did not harm the firstborn sons of the Israelites, who had marked their doorposts with blood.

4 That night Pharaoh sent for Moses and Aaron. "Get out, you and your people!" Pharaoh cried. "Leave my country, and worship the Lord as you wish. Take your animals and leave!"

5 All the Egyptians urged the Israelites to hurry and get out of the country. "We will all be dead if you don't." They gave the Israelites gold and silver jewelry and fine clothing.

6 The Israelites set out on foot. There were about 600,000 men, not counting the women and children. They also took their animals and many other people with them.

7 The Israelites had lived in Egypt for 430 years. On the day the 430 years ended, all the tribes of the Lord's people left Egypt.

8 Moses took with him the body of Joseph, who had ruled Egypt years before. Before he died, Joseph had made the Israelites promise to take along his remains when they left Egypt.

9 The Lord did not lead them through the land of the fierce Philistines, lest they be afraid and want to return to Egypt. Instead, he led them through the desert toward the Red Sea.

10 During the day the Lord went in front of them in a pillar of cloud to show them the way, and during the night he went in front of them in a pillar of fire. They could travel night and day.

11 When the Pharaoh was told that the people had escaped, he changed his mind. He and his officials said, "What have we done? The Israelites have escaped! We have lost our slaves!"

12 The Israelites moved closer to the Red Sea. Suddenly they saw Pharaoh and 600 soldiers coming toward them in war chariots. The Israelites were terrified!

Israel Crosses the Red Sea

1 The Israelites were now camped near the Red Sea. Suddenly they discovered that Pharaoh and his soldiers in their war chariots were about to catch up with them!

2 The frightened Israelites cried out to the Lord for help. They were angry with Moses for leading them out of Egypt only to let them be killed in the desert.

3 But Moses said, "Don't be afraid! Stand your ground, and you will see what the Lord will do to save you today. The Lord will fight for you, and all you have to do is keep still."

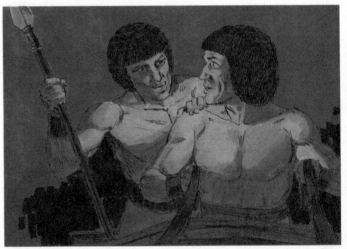

4 Then the Lord moved the pillar of cloud between the Israelites and the Egyptians. The cloud made it so dark that the army of Egypt could not come near the Israelites all night.

5 Moses, as the Lord had instructed, held out his hand over the sea. Then the Lord sent a strong east wind which blew all night and turned the sea into dry land.

6 The water was divided, and the Israelites walked through the sea on dry ground, with walls of water on both sides!

7 The army of Egypt chased them into the sea with all their horses, chariots, and drivers. But the wheels of their chariots got stuck so that they could barely move.

8 Just before dawn, the Lord threw the army of Egypt into panic. They said, "The Lord is fighting for the Israelites against us. Let's get out of here!"

9 Again the Lord told Moses to hold his hand over the sea, and the water returned to its normal level. The Egyptians' chariots were covered with water and the entire army drowned.

10 The Israelites stood in awe of the power of the Lord which had saved them from the Egyptians. They put their trust in the Lord and his servant Moses.

11 Moses and the people sang to the Lord their God: "Lord, who among the gods is like you? Who can work miracles and mighty acts like yours?"

12 The women celebrated as Moses' sister Miriam sang: "Sing to the Lord for his glorious victory; he has thrown the horses and their riders into the sea."

God Provides for His People

1 After the Lord rescued them from the Egyptians, the Israelites traveled on into the desert of Shur. For three days they could find no water at all.

2 Then at Marah they found water, but it was so bitter that they could not drink it. Moses prayed to the Lord, who showed him how to work a miracle that made the water fit to drink.

3 The people continued on to the desert of Sin. There they complained to Moses and Aaron because they had nothing to eat. "We wish the Lord had killed us in Egypt. You're letting us starve."

4 The Lord said to Moses, "I am going to cause food to rain down from heaven for all of you. Each day the people must gather enough for that day. On the sixth day, they must gather twice as much."

5 That evening a flock of quails flew into the camp, and in the morning dew was all around. The dew evaporated, leaving something thin and flaky that tasted like cakes made with honey.

6 The Israelites named this food "manna." Moses said, "This is the food that the Lord has given you. Gather two quarts for each member of your family. But don't keep any overnight."

7 Some people paid no attention and saved part of it. In the morning it was full of worms and smelled rotten. From then on, they gathered only what they needed. The rest melted in the sun.

8 Every evening the Israelites had meat from the quails that flew into the camp. In the morning they had manna for bread. On the seventh day of the week, they rested as God had commanded.

9 The extra amount gathered on the sixth day did not spoil or get worms but was fine the next morning. Then Moses said, "Eat this today, for today is a day of rest dedicated to the Lord."

10 Some of the people ignored Moses' command to collect none on the seventh day. They went out to look for manna and found nothing. The Lord was angry with them for not obeying Moses.

11 Later the Lord commanded the Israelites to save some of the manna so that they could show their descendants what God had provided them to eat in the desert.

12 The Israelites ate manna for the next forty years. Later, when they entered the land of Canaan, they could settle down and grow their own food.

Moses on Mount Sinai

■ The Israelites left the desert of Sin, where the Lord sent them quail and manna for food. They moved from one place to another at the command of the Lord.

2 Three months after they had left Egypt, the Israelites came to the desert of Sinai. There, at the foot of Mount Sinai, they set up camp. Moses went up on the mountain to meet with God.

3 The Lord gave Moses a message for the Israelites: "You saw what I, the Lord, did to the Egyptians and how I carried you as an eagle carries her young on her wings, and brought you here."

4 Then the Lord made a covenant, or agreement, with them. "If you obey me and keep my covenant," he said, "you will be my people. All the earth is mine, but you will be my chosen people."

5 So Moses went down and told the leaders of the people everything that the Lord had commanded him. Then all the people answered together, "We will do everything that the Lord has said."

6 Moses reported this to God. Then the Lord said to Moses, "I will come to you in a thick cloud so that the people will hear me speaking with you and will believe you from now on."

7 "Tell the people to spend today and tomorrow purifying themselves for worship. On the day after tomorrow, I will come down on Mount Sinai, where all the people can see me."

8 "Mark a boundary around the mountain that the people must not cross. Tell them not to go up the mountain or even get near it. If anyone sets foot on it, he must be put to death."

9 Moses came down and told the Israelites to get ready to worship God. "Be ready by the day after tomorrow," he said. "When the trumpet sounds, we must go to the mountain."

10 On the morning of the third day, there was thunder and lightning. A thick cloud of smoke covered the mountain, and a trumpet blast was heard. All the people trembled with fear.

11 Moses led them out of the camp to meet God. They stood at the foot of the mountain. All the people trembled violently, as the trumpet sounds got louder and louder.

12 Then the Lord called Moses back up to the mountain. God was now ready to give Israel the law of his covenant.

The Golden Calf

1 Moses was on Mount Sinai forty days and forty nights while God wrote on stone tablets ten important commandments for his people.

2 The people grew restless. "We don't know what has happened to Moses," they said to Aaron. "Make us a god to lead us." So Aaron had them bring all their gold earrings to him.

3 Aaron melted the gold and molded a golden calf. The people shouted, "This is our god, who led us out of Egypt!" They brought sacrifices and began eating, drinking, singing, and dancing.

4 The Lord said to Moses on the mountain, "Hurry back to the camp. Your people, whom you led out of Egypt, have sinned and rejected me. They have made an idol and are worshiping it."

5 God was so angry that he wanted to destroy them. But Moses pleaded, "Do not destroy the people. Remember your promises to Abraham, Isaac, and Jacob." So God changed his mind.

6 Moses went down the mountain with the two stone tablets containing the Ten Commandments. When he saw the golden calf and the people dancing, he threw down the tablets and broke them.

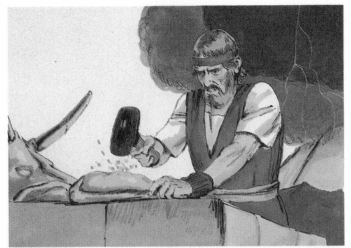

7 Moses took the image the people had made and melted it. He ground it into fine powder. Then he mixed it with water and made the people of Israel drink it.

8 When Moses asked Aaron why he had done such a terrible thing, Aaron blamed it on the people. He also gave this excuse: "I threw the ornaments into the fire, and out came this calf!"

9 The Lord was angry at the people's sin. At his command, the Levites went through the camp that day and killed about 3,000 of the Israelites who had disobeyed the Lord.

10 Then the Lord told Moses to cut two more stone tablets and bring them to the top of the mountain. Once again the Ten Commandments were written on the stone tablets.

11 After forty days and forty nights, Moses delivered the laws of the Lord to the people. The first four commands told the people how to respect and worship God and him alone.

12 The last six commands told the people of their duties to one another: not to steal, lie, covet, or kill; to honor their parents and be true to their mates. The people promised to obey the Lord.

The Tabernacle

1 The Lord said to Moses, "The people must make a Tabernacle, a sacred tent for me, so I may live among them. Make it by the plan I will show you." So the people made the Tabernacle.

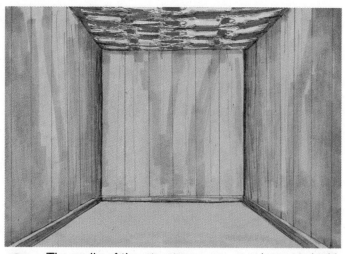

2 The walls of the structure were wood covered with gold and set in sockets of silver. The first covering was an embroidered curtain of linen woven with blue, purple, and red thread.

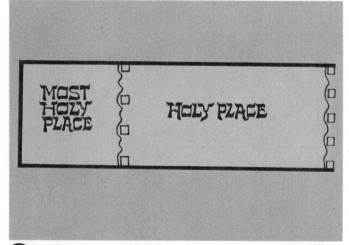

3 The Tabernacle held two rooms, called the "Holy Place" and the "Most Holy Place." The outer coverings of the Tabernacle had three layers: goat hair cloth, ram skins, and fine leather.

4 Inside the Most Holy Place was a very important item. It was the Ark of the Covenant, or Covenant Box. In it were kept the two stone tablets containing the Ten Commandments.

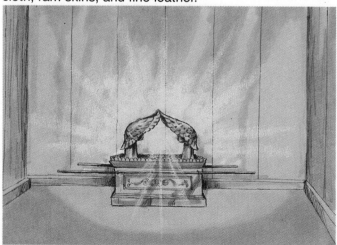

5 The lid of the Covenant Box was made of pure gold. On top of it were two angels whose wings covered the lid. God said, "I will meet you there, and from above the lid I will give my laws."

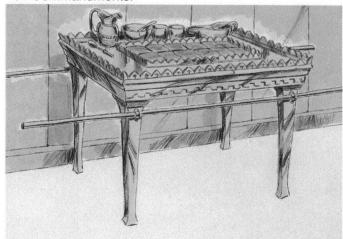

6 A table made of wood and covered with gold was placed in the Holy Place against the north wall. On it were the bread offering and the golden cups and bowls for the wine offering.

7 A lampstand made of gold and decorated with golden almond blossoms was also in the Holy Place. Every evening Aaron, the High Priest, lit its seven lamps and let them burn until morning.

8 The gold incense altar was placed in the Holy Place next to the curtain that divided the two rooms. Each evening and each morning the priests burned sweet-smelling incense on it.

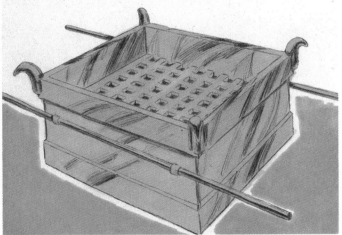

9 Outside in the courtyard was the altar for burnt offerings. It was made of wood and covered with bronze. The priests burned a lamb on it every morning and evening as a sacrifice.

10 Between the altar and the tent was a bronze basin containing water, which the priests used to wash their hands and feet before offering sacrifices and before entering the tent.

11 Forming a spacious courtyard around the tent was a fence—a curtain of fine linen supported by bronze posts. This fence and the tent could be taken down and folded up.

12 The Covenant Box, the altar, and the table had rings for carrying-poles. Thus the Tabernacle could be moved as the people of Israel moved from one place to another.

The Spies Sent to Canaan

1 The Lord spoke to Moses in the wilderness of Paran: "Choose a leader from each of the tribes and send them to explore the land of Canaan, which I have promised to give them."

2 Moses chose twelve men and said to them, "Find out how good the land is and how strong the people are. Find out if their cities are fortified." Then he sent the spies on to Canaan.

3 The spies returned after exploring the land for forty days. "The land is rich and fertile," they said, "but the people there are strong and their cities are well fortified."

4 However, one of the spies, Caleb, said, "We should attack now and take the land. We are strong enough to conquer it." Ten of the spies said, "No, the people there are too powerful."

5 "The land will not be good for us," these spies told the Israelites. "And the people are giants. We felt as small as grasshoppers, and that is how we must have looked to them."

6 All night long the people complained to Moses. "It would have been better to die in Egypt! If we do go to this land, we'll be killed! Let's choose a new leader and go back to Egypt!"

7 But Caleb and Joshua, the two faithful spies, said to the people, "The land we explored is an excellent one. With God's help, we can conquer the people easily! Don't be afraid!"

8 But the people were about to stone the two spies when the light of God appeared over the Tabernacle. God said, "How much longer will these people refuse to trust in me? I will destroy them!"

9 Moses prayed, and the Lord changed his mind. But God said, "None of the unfaithful will live to enter the land. You will wander around for forty years, until the last of you is dead."

10 The ten spies who had spread the false report were struck with a disease and died. But Joshua and Caleb, who had been faithful, were not harmed.

11 When the people learned what the Lord had said, they decided to leave right away for Canaan. Moses warned them, saying, "The Lord will not be with you. You will die in battle."

12 The people paid no attention to Moses. But as Moses had said, they were defeated and chased away by the Canaanites. Without the Lord's help, they could not enter Canaan.

The Last Days of Moses

1 The people of Israel had wandered for forty years in the wilderness. Now, at last, they were to enter the land God had promised them. For Moses the joy was mixed with disappointment.

2 Moses had failed to honor the Lord before the people when they were in the wilderness of Sin. For that reason, God would not permit Moses to enter the promised land with the rest of the people of Israel.

3 Since he himself could not enter Canaan, Moses asked the Lord to appoint someone in his place to lead the people and to command them in battle, so the Israelites would not be like sheep without a shepherd.

4 The Lord chose Joshua the son of Nun to be the next leader. Joshua was one of the twelve spies who spied out Canaan. Moses had Joshua stand before the people and gave him authority to be their leader.

5 Moses really wanted to enter the promised land. He prayed that God would let him. But God said, "That's enough! Don't mention this again! You may see the land from afar, but you may not enter it."

6 So Moses said to Joshua, "You are the one who will lead these people into the land the Lord promised our ancestors. The Lord himself will lead you and be with you, so do not lose courage or be afraid."

7 Then Moses climbed the mountains east of Jericho and looked out over all the land. The Lord said, "This is the land I promised Abraham, Isaac, and Jacob I would give to their descendants."

8 After Moses saw the promised land, he died and God buried him in the land of Moab. He was 120 years old when he died, but he was still strong as ever and his eyesight was good.

9 The Israelites mourned for Moses for thirty days there in the plains of Moab.

10 There has never been another prophet in Israel like Moses. The Lord spoke with him face to face. No other prophet has ever done miracles like the Lord sent Moses to perform against the king of Egypt.

11 Joshua, Moses' successor, was filled with wisdom. The people of Israel obeyed Joshua and kept the commands the Lord had given through Moses.

12 With the death of Moses, one chapter in the history of Israel ends and a new one begins. God has kept many of his promises to Abraham, Isaac, and Jacob. Now he is ready to fulfill the remaining promises.

Joshua Sends Out Spies

1 After the death of Moses, the Lord said to Joshua the son of Nun, "Get ready to lead the people of Israel across the Jordan into the land that I have promised to give them."

2 So Joshua sent two spies from the camp with orders to secretly explore the land of Canaan, especially the city of Jericho.

3 When the spies got to Jericho, they stayed the night in the house of a woman named Rahab. She took them up on her roof and hid them under stalks of flax that she had put there to dry.

4 Word reached the king of Jericho that Israelite spies had entered Rahab's house. He sent a message to her: "The men in your house have come to spy on our country! Bring them out!"

5 Rahab replied, "Some men did come to my house, but I don't know where they have gone. They left at sundown— if you hurry you can catch them." So the king's men left to search for the spies.

6 Before the spies went to sleep that night, Rahab said, "I know the Lord has given you this land. Now swear to me that you will treat my family as I have treated you. Don't let them be killed!"

7 The two men answered, "If you do not tell anyone what we have been doing, we promise you that when the Lord gives us this land, we will treat you well."

8 Rahab's house was built into the city wall, so she helped the spies escape by letting them down from the window by a rope. She also told the spies what to do so the king's men would not find them.

9 The two spies said to Rahab, "We will keep our promise to you. Tie this red cord to the window. Make sure that when we attack your relatives are all in your house; there they will be safe."

10 "But if you tell anyone what we have been doing," they added, "then we will not have to keep our promise." Rahab agreed, and after they left she tied the red cord to her window.

11 The two spies hid in the hills for three days, as Rahab had advised. The king's men looked all over the countryside for them but finally gave up and returned to Jericho.

12 Then the spies left the hills and crossed the Jordan to return to their camp. They told Joshua all that had happened and then said, "We are sure that the Lord has given us the entire country!"

The Israelites Enter Canaan

1 The very next morning after the two spies returned, Joshua had the people of Israel move their camp to a place beside the Jordan River. There they waited to cross the river.

2 The leaders went through the camp telling the people that when the priests with the Covenant Box moved, they were to follow at a distance of about half a mile. Then Joshua told the priests to start out.

3 As was usual at harvest time, the river was so full that it overflowed its banks. But when the priests carrying the Covenant Box stepped into the water, the river stopped flowing and the water piled up upstream!

4 No water flowed down to the Dead Sea. So the priests with the Covenant Box stood in the middle of the dry riverbed, and the people of Israel walked across the Jordan on dry ground!

5 Joshua chose twelve men and said to them, "Each of you take a stone from the middle of the riverbed and carry it to the place we are going to camp." They did so and put the stones down there.

6 After all the people were safe, Joshua told the priests with the Covenant Box to come out of the riverbed. As soon as they did, the waters began to flow and the river flooded its banks again!

7 They made camp at Gilgal, east of Jericho, and there Joshua set up the twelve stones taken from the Jordan. He said, "When your children ask you what these stones mean, tell them what happened here."

8 "Tell them that the Lord your God dried up the Jordan for you, just as he dried up the Red Sea. Then everyone will know that the Lord is a mighty God, and you will honor the Lord forever."

9 News of how the Lord had dried up the Jordan so the people of Israel could cross it reached all the kings in Canaan, and they were afraid of the Israelites.

10 What the Lord did through Joshua that day made the people of Israel consider Joshua a great man. They knew the Lord was with him. They held him in honor all his life, just as they had Moses.

11 The Lord ordered that all the boys and men be circumcised there at Gilgal. No one had been circumcised during the last forty years. On the fourteenth day of the month, the Israelites celebrated the Passover.

12 The next day they ate food grown in Canaan for the first time! The manna stopped falling, and the Israelites never had any more. From that time on they ate food grown in Canaan.

The Battle of Jericho

1 The people of Jericho knew that Israelite spies had been in their city, and they were very worried. After the spies escaped, no one was permitted to go in or out of the city.

2 The Lord said to Joshua, "I have delivered Jericho into your hands." He told Joshua to have seven priests with trumpets of rams' horns march ahead of the priests carrying the Covenant Box.

3 So Joshua ordered his men to march around the city of Jericho. Some of the soldiers marched in front of the priests with the trumpets, and the rest marched behind the Covenant Box.

4 As they marched around the city, the priests blew on their trumpets, but the soldiers kept silent, as Joshua had ordered. They circled the city one time and then returned to their camp, where they spent the night.

5 Each day for six days Joshua and his men marched around Jericho one time, making no sound except for that of the rams' horn trumpets.

6 But on the seventh day they got up at daybreak and marched around the city *seven* times! On the last time around Joshua said to his men, "Shout! The Lord has given you the city!"

7 So the priests blew one long note on the trumpets and all the soldiers gave a great shout—and the walls of Jericho fell down! Immediately Joshua's men charged straight in and captured the city.

8 With their swords the Israelite soldiers killed everyone in the city—both men and women, young and old. They even killed the cattle, sheep, and donkeys, as Joshua ordered them to do.

9 Only Rahab and her family were spared. The two spies went to the house with the red cord tied to the window and led out Rahab and her family to a safe place. Thus they kept their promise to her.

10 Joshua warned the soldiers, "Don't take anything from the city. Everything metal must be set apart for the Lord. Anyone who takes something for himself will bring trouble upon our people."

11 Then the Israelites set fire to the city and burned it to the ground, along with everything left in it. At that time Joshua gave this warning: "Anyone who tries to rebuild this city will be under the Lord's curse."

12 Afterwards, Joshua put the silver and gold and things made of bronze and iron in the treasury of the Lord's house. Thus the Lord was with Joshua and his fame spread throughout the land.

The Sun Stands Still

1 After Jericho, the Israelites destroyed the city of Ai. The news spread throughout Canaan. Then came word that the city of Gibeon had made a peace treaty with the Israelites!

2 When Adonizedek the king of Jerusalem heard that, he became alarmed. Gibeon was a large city and its men were good fighters. Now they might fight on the Israelites' side against the other cities of Canaan.

3 So Adonizedek contacted the kings of the cities of Hebron, Jarmuth, Lachish, and Eglon, and they agreed to help him. These five kings joined forces and attacked the city of Gibeon.

4 Surrounded, the men of Gibeon sent urgent word to Joshua at his camp in Gilgal: "All the Amorite kings in the hill country have attacked us! Come at once and help us! Do not abandon us!"

5 Joshua and his army marched all night. When they reached Gibeon, they made a surprise attack on the Amorites. The Amorites panicked and many of them were killed there at Gibeon.

6 Others fled, pursued by the Israelites. Many of the fleeing Amorites were killed by large hailstones which fell on them between the mountain pass at Beth Horon and the city of Azekah.

7 That day Joshua prayed, and the Lord made the sun stand still! The sun did not go down for a whole day, until Israel conquered its enemies. Never before or since has there been a day like that!

8 Someone came to Joshua and said, "The five Amorite kings have escaped and are hiding in a cave at Makkedah." Joshua ordered that large stones be put in front of the cave so the kings could not get out.

9 The Israelites chased down the Amorites and killed most of them. Only a few reached the safety of their city walls. Then all of Joshua's men came back safely to him at the camp at Makkedah.

10 Joshua ordered the cave opened and the five kings brought to him. He told his officers to put their feet on the necks of the kings, and said, "This is what the Lord will do to your enemies."

11 Then Joshua killed the kings and hanged each of them on a tree. At sundown their bodies were taken down and thrown into the cave where they had tried to hide. The cave was sealed with large stones.

12 Next Joshua attacked the cities of Makkedah, Libnah, Lachish, Eglon, Hebron, and Debir. Everyone in each city was put to death, as the Lord had commanded. Then Joshua and his army returned to Gilgal.

Deborah

1 Joshua bravely led the people until they had conquered the land of Canaan. Before he died, he reminded the Israelites of their covenant with the Lord. The people promised to obey God.

2 But the people had not destroyed all the Canaanites' idols. Before long, some of them began to worship Baal and the gods of the Canaanites. Thus Israel became unfaithful to the Lord.

3 The Lord let Jabin, king of Hazor, conquer the disobedient people of Israel. Jabin was very cruel, and he treated the Israelites harshly for twenty years. Then Israel began to cry out to God for help.

4 There was a woman named Deborah, who was not only a prophetess but also a judge. She often sat under a certain palm tree near Bethel. People came there to ask her help in settling problems.

5 One day, Deborah sent for a man named Barak. She said, "The Lord has ordered you to take soldiers and fight against Jabin's army. He has iron chariots, but you will defeat him."

6 Barak replied, "I will go only if you go with me." She answered, "I'll go, but you will not get credit for the victory. God will hand over Sisera, commander of Jabin's army, to a woman."

7 So Deborah and Barak went to Kedesh. From there Barak led ten thousand Israelite soldiers to Mount Tabor. When Sisera heard this, he attacked with his army and 900 iron chariots.

8 Then Deborah said, "Go, Barak! Today the Lord has given you victory over Sisera!" Barak attacked, and the Lord threw Sisera's army into confusion. The Israelites killed them all!

9 However, Sisera himself escaped on foot. He came to the tent of Jael—the wife of a man distantly related to Moses! Jael helped Sisera hide inside her tent. She even gave him milk when he was thirsty.

10 Sisera was very tired and fell sound asleep. Then Jael took a hammer and a tent peg and slipped up beside Sisera. She drove the tent peg through the side of his head and into the ground!

11 When Barak came looking for Sisera, Jael said, "I'll show you the man you are looking for." Inside her tent Barak found the body of Sisera, with the tent peg driven through his head.

12 On that very day, Deborah and Barak sang praise to the Lord: "So may all your enemies die, O Lord, but may your friends shine like the rising sun!" Afterwards, there was peace for about forty years.

God Chooses Gideon

1 Once again the people of Israel sinned against the Lord by worshiping the gods of the Canaanites. To punish the Israelites, God let the people of Midian rule over them and ruin their land.

2 Every year when the Israelites planted their grain, the Midianites came like a cloud of locusts and attacked them. They destroyed the grain and took away their sheep and cattle, leaving nothing for the Israelites.

3 The Israelites were completely helpless against the Midianites, and so they hid in caves and other safe places in the hills. Finally, after seven years, they cried out to the Lord for help against the Midianites.

4 Then the angel of the Lord spoke to Gideon the son of Joash in the village of Ophrah: "Go, rescue Israel from the Midianites. I myself am sending you." The Lord told Gideon what to do first.

5 That night—for he was afraid of being seen—Gideon and his servants tore down his father's altar to the god Baal. They cut down the pole beside it, which was a symbol of the goddess Asherah.

6 Then Gideon built a new altar to the Lord at that same place. He offered a bull as a sacrifice to God. Gideon used the Asherah pole as firewood to burn the sacrifice.

7 The next morning the people were furious and wanted to kill Gideon. But Gideon's father said, "Are you defending Baal? If Baal is a god, let him defend himself." So they let Gideon alone.

8 Then news came that the Midianites and Amalekites had crossed the Jordan River into the Jezreel valley. Gideon sent messengers to the men of Israel to come and help fight them.

9 Gideon asked God for signs so he could be sure of God's help. First, God made some wool wet with dew while the ground around it was dry. Then he made the wool dry while the ground was wet.

10 God said to Gideon, "You have so many men that you may think you have won this victory by yourselves. Send away anyone who is afraid." Gideon did so, but still 10,000 men remained.

11 So God said, "Take the men to the stream and send home all who get down on their knees to drink." Then only 300 men were left. God said, "I will give you victory over the Midianites with only 300 men."

12 God sent Gideon to spy on the enemy camp. In the darkness, Gideon crept close and heard a soldier explaining his friend's dream: "It means that God has given the victory to Gideon!"

Gideon's Victory over Midian

1 Hiding in the darkness, Gideon overheard an enemy soldier say that Israel would defeat the Midianite army. So Gideon returned to his camp and prepared for battle that very night.

2 Gideon followed God's directions: he divided his men into three groups of 100 men each. Then he gave each man a trumpet and a jar with a torch in it. The three groups took positions around the enemy camp.

3 Just after the guard was changed for the midnight watch, the three groups of Israelite soldiers blew their trumpets and broke the jars they were holding. Their torches blazed in the night.

4 With their torches in their left hands and the trumpets in their right, the Israelites shouted, "A sword for the Lord and for Gideon!" The Midianites panicked. They attacked each other and ran away.

5 Gideon immediately sent messengers throughout the hill country. They called out other Israelites to help chase and destroy the fleeing Midianites.

6 His men were now tired and hungry from fighting, so Gideon asked the people of Succoth and Penuel for food. But they refused, fearing that the Midianites might win and punish them for helping Israel.

7 Already 120,000 Midianites had been killed. Now Gideon defeated the last 15,000 of the enemy in a surprise attack at Karkor. The kings Zebah and Zalmunna were taken captive and later executed.

8 Then Gideon returned to the towns that had refused to help the Israelites during the battle. Gideon ordered his men to punish the leaders of Succoth with thorns and briars and to kill the men of Penuel.

9 After this victory, the Israelites said to Gideon: "You have saved us from our enemies the Midianites. You be our ruler! And your sons can rule after you."

10 But Gideon refused, saying, "Only the Lord shall rule over you." But he did have a request: "Give me all the gold earrings you took from the Midianites." The people were glad to do so.

11 Gideon took the gold and made an object, which he placed in his hometown, Ophrah. The Israelites sinned against God by worshiping this object, and it proved to be a real problem for Gideon and his family.

12 After defeating the Midianites, Israel lived in peace for forty years. But after Gideon died, the Israelites became unfaithful to the Lord who had saved them. They forgot the Lord and worshiped Baal again.

Ruth Is Loyal

1 In the days when Israel was still ruled by judges — that is, before there was a king — there was a famine in the land.

2 An Israelite named Elimelech, who lived in Bethlehem of Judah, decided to take his wife and two sons and live for a while in the land of Moab, where there was food.

3 While living in Moab, Elimelech died. Naomi was left alone with her two sons. After a time, the sons married Moabite girls named Orpah and Ruth.

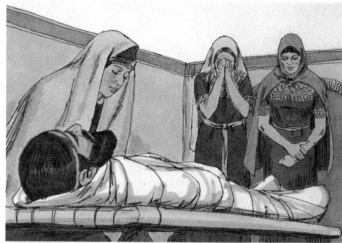

4 About ten years later the two sons also died. Now Naomi was left without husband or sons — just two foreign daughters-in-law.

5 Time — and the famine — passed. Naomi heard that the Lord had blessed the Israelites with good crops. She decided to take her daughters-in-law and return to her home in Bethlehem.

6 On the way, Naomi changed her mind. "Go back to your homes," she said. "May the Lord be as good to you as you have been to me. May you marry again and have your own homes."

7 Naomi then kissed them goodbye, but they began to cry and said, "No! We will go with you!" But Naomi said, "I am too old to have other sons for you to marry. You must go home."

8 Again they started crying. Then Orpah kissed her mother-in-law and went back to the home of her parents. Ruth, however, kept holding onto Naomi.

9 "Ruth, your sister-in-law has gone back to her people and to her gods," said Naomi. "Go back with her."

10 Ruth said: "Don't ask me to leave you! Wherever you go, I will go; wherever you live, I will live. Your people will be my people, and your God will be my God. Wherever you die, I will die."

11 Seeing that Ruth was determined to go with her, Naomi said nothing more. Finally they arrived at Bethlehem. Everyone was very excited to see them and exclaimed, "Is it really Naomi?"

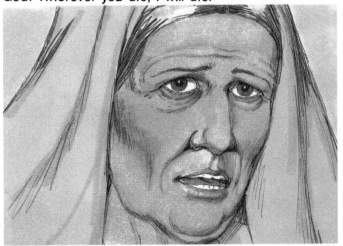

12 Naomi said, "Don't call me 'Naomi' (pleasant) but call me 'Mara' (bitter), because God has made my life bitter. When I left here, I had plenty, but the Lord has brought me back without a thing."

Boaz Is Kind

1 After her husband and two sons died, Naomi returned from Moab to Bethlehem of Judah. She and her daughter-in-law Ruth arrived just at the beginning of the barley harvest.

2 Since there was no man to provide for them, Ruth said to Naomi, "Let me go to the fields to gather the grain that the workers leave." So with Naomi's permission, Ruth went out to the fields.

3 After Ruth had been gathering awhile, the owner of the field came there. It so happened that this field was owned by a man named Boaz, who was a relative of Naomi's dead husband.

4 When Boaz noticed Ruth, he asked the man in charge about her. The man replied, "She asked to gather the grain the workers miss. She worked all morning and has just stopped to rest."

5 Boaz went over to Ruth. "Why don't you stay in my field?" he suggested. "Work close to the women. My men won't bother you, and when you get thirsty they will give you water."

6 Ruth bowed down with her face touching the ground. She exclaimed, "Why should you be so concerned about me, a foreigner?"

7 Boaz answered, "I have heard about your kindness to Naomi. I know how you left your home and came to live among strangers. May the Lord reward you for what you have done."

8 At lunch time, Boaz said to Ruth, "Come and eat with us." So she sat with the workers and Boaz and ate all the bread and barley grain she wanted.

9 After Ruth went back to work, Boaz gave orders to his workers: "Let her gather all she needs. And pull out some heads of grain from the bundles and leave them for her to pick up."

10 That evening when Ruth beat out the gathered grain, she found that she had about twenty-five pounds of it. Naomi was surprised and said, "From whose field did you get so much grain?"

11 Ruth told her the field belonged to Boaz. Naomi cried, "The Lord always keeps his promise to the living and the dead! That man is a relative who is responsible for taking care of us!"

12 Naomi was very happy that Boaz had told Ruth to keep on gathering in his field. Ruth would be safe there. So Ruth worked in Boaz's field until all the barley and wheat had been harvested.

Ruth Marries Boaz

1 Ruth and Naomi continued to live on the grain which Ruth gathered by following behind the workers in Boaz's field. Boaz made sure that his workers left plenty for Ruth to gather.

2 As time passed, Naomi decided she should find a husband for Ruth. Naomi thought up a plan concerning Boaz, who was a close relative, and Ruth agreed to do as Naomi said.

3 So that evening Ruth went to the place where Boaz was threshing the barley, but she did not let him see her. After he ate and drank, he lay down beside the pile of barley to sleep.

4 When she was sure Boaz was sound asleep, Ruth slipped over quietly and lay down at his feet. During the night he suddenly woke up and discovered her beside him. "Who is it?" he asked.

5 "It's your servant Ruth. Since you are my close relative, you are responsible for taking care of me. So please marry me."

6 Boaz said, "This loyalty to your husband's family is even greater than the loyalty you've shown to Naomi. I will do what you ask, but first I must talk to a man who is your closest relative."

7 So Ruth stayed beside him that night. The next morning Boaz went to the meeting place at the town gate. When he found the close relative, he had him sit down with ten of the town leaders.

8 Then Boaz explained: "Naomi wants to sell the field that belonged to Elimelech. Since you are the closest relative, you have the first chance to buy it. But if you don't want it, I do."

9 The man replied, "I will buy it." So Boaz said, "Very well, but you should know that whoever buys the field also buys Ruth, the Moabite widow, so that the land will remain in the dead man's family."

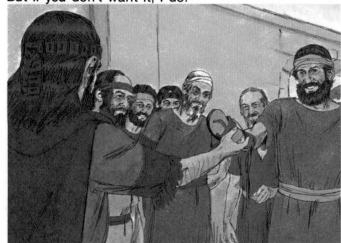

10 "Then you buy it," the man said to Boaz. "I give up my claim on it, because my own children could not inherit it." He took off his sandal and gave it to Boaz, as was the custom when trading land.

11 Then Boaz said to the town leaders, "You are all witnesses of this." "Yes, we are," they replied. "And may the Lord make your wife like Rachel and Leah, who bore Jacob many children."

12 So Boaz married Ruth, the loyal Moabite woman. In time they had a baby boy, whom they named Obed. This Obed grew up to become the grandfather of David, the king of all Israel.

Samson the Nazirite

1 The Israelites sinned against the Lord; to punish them, God let the Philistines rule over them for forty years.

2 At that time there was a certain woman who had no children. She was very surprised when an angel appeared to her one day and said, "You will soon become the mother of a baby boy."

3 The angel added: "Be sure not to drink any wine or eat any forbidden food. Don't ever cut the boy's hair, for he will be dedicated to God as a Nazirite from the day he is born."

4 In time the woman did, indeed, give birth to a son, whom she and her husband named Samson. The child grew, and the Lord blessed him.

5 One day after he was grown, Samson made a trip to Timnah. When he got back home, he said to his parents, "I saw a Philistine girl over at Timnah. I want you to get her for my wife."

6 His parents were, of course, upset, and said, "Why do you have to marry a Philistine? Can't you find a nice girl among our own people?" But Samson would not listen to them.

7 On the way to Timnah Samson killed a lion, but he told no one about it. Returning a few days later for his wedding, Samson found that some bees had made honey in the body of the lion.

8 Samson bet thirty men each a set of clothes that they could not explain this riddle before the feast's end: "Out of the eater came something to eat; out of the strong came something sweet."

9 On the fourth day of the wedding feast they said to Samson's wife: "Get your husband to tell what the riddle means. If you don't, we'll burn your father's house and you with it!"

10 She went to Samson and said, "You don't love me! You told my friends a riddle and didn't tell me what it means!" She cried every day until on the last day Samson told her its meaning.

11 Just before sundown, the young men came to him and said, "What could be sweeter than honey or stronger than a lion?" Samson was furious that his wife had told them the answer.

12 Samson went to Ashkelon and he killed thirty men. He gave their clothes to the young men who had answered his riddle. Then he returned to his home in great anger — without his new bride.

Samson and the Philistines

1 When the young Philistine men guessed the meaning of his riddle, Samson knew his bride had betrayed him. He returned in anger to his father's house without her.

2 Later Samson tried to visit his wife, but her father said, "I thought you hated her, so I gave her to your friend. Her younger sister is prettier anyway. You can have her instead."

3 But Samson said, "This time I've got a right to get even with the Philistines!" So he went out and caught 300 foxes, tied their tails together in pairs, and fastened torches in the knots.

4 Then he set fire to the torches and let the foxes run through the fields of the Philistines. All the wheat still in the fields was burned up, and the olive orchards were ruined, too.

5 When the Philistines found out that Samson had done this because his father-in-law had given his wife to a friend, the Philistines went and burned Samson's wife and her father to death.

6 Samson was enraged. "I'm going to pay you back for what you've done!" he swore. He attacked the Philistines and killed many of them. Afterwards, he went and lived in a cave at Etam.

7 Soon the Philistines attacked the town of Lehi in Judah. The men of Judah asked, "Why have you attacked us?" They found out that the Philistines wanted to take Samson prisoner.

8 Some men of Judah went to the cave and said to Samson, "What have you done? Don't you know the Philistines are our rulers?" Samson replied, "I just did to them what they did to me."

9 The men told Samson they were going to give him over to the Philistines. Samson made them promise they would not kill him and then let them tie him up with two new ropes.

10 At Lehi, the Philistines came running toward Samson. Suddenly the Spirit of the Lord made him strong, and he broke the ropes around his arms and hands as if they were burnt thread.

11 Looking about, he found the jawbone of a donkey that had recently died. Samson used the jawbone as a weapon and with it killed 1,000 Philistines.

12 During the twenty years that he led Israel, Samson had other troubles with the Philistines. The most famous of these happened after Samson fell in love with a woman named Delilah.

Samson and Delilah

1 Delilah was a Philistine woman from the valley of Sorek. Samson loved her, though the Philistines were his enemies.

2 One day five Philistine kings came to her and said, "Get Samson to tell why he is so strong and how we can overpower him. Each of us will give you 1,100 pieces of silver if you do."

3 So Delilah said to Samson, "What makes you so strong? If someone wanted to make you helpless, how could he do it?" He replied, "If I were tied up with seven new bowstrings, I'd be helpless."

4 So she tied Samson with seven new bowstrings and then shouted, "Samson! The Philistines are coming!" Samson jumped up and broke the bowstrings just as if they were thread.

5 Delilah was angry. "You're making a fool of me!" she said. "Now tell me the truth." But each time he gave her an answer, she found out when she tested it that he had not told her the truth.

6 Day after day she kept asking, "Why are you so strong?" Finally Samson told her the truth. "I am a Nazirite," he said. "If my hair is ever cut, I will lose my strength."

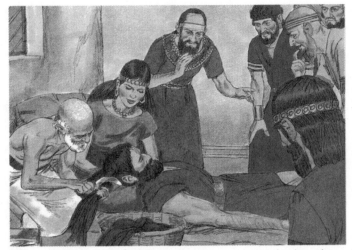

7 Delilah got Samson to go to sleep in her lap. Then a man came in and cut off Samson's hair. This time Samson was unable to escape when he woke up, for the Lord had left him.

8 The Philistines tied up Samson with chains and put out his eyes. They took him to Gaza, where they put him to work grinding grain at a mill. During this time, Samson's hair began to grow back.

9 The Philistine kings held a celebration to offer a sacrifice to Dagon, their god, for giving them victory over Samson. The temple was packed with about 3,000 men and women.

10 When the now blind Samson was brought in to entertain them, the Philistines sang: "Dagon has given us victory over our enemy, who ruined our land and killed many of our people."

11 Samson told the boy who was leading him to take him to the main columns that held up the temple. Then he prayed, "Lord, give me my strength so that I can get even with the Philistines."

12 Samson pushed against the columns with all his might and the building fell down on everyone. Samson died with them, but he killed more Philistines that day than he had in all his life.

Samuel the Prophet

1 Every year a man named Elkanah took his family to Shiloh to offer sacrifices at the Tabernacle of the Lord. Hophni and Phinehas, the sons of Eli, were the priests in charge there.

2 After the sacrifices one year, Elkanah's wife Hannah prayed for a son. She promised that if God answered her prayer, she would dedicate her son to the Lord for all of his life.

3 In time Hannah had a son, whom she named Samuel. When he was about three years old, Hannah took him to Eli at Shiloh. She said, "I have come to give my son to the Lord, as I promised."

4 The sons of Eli were wicked men who did not obey the Lord, even though they were priests. They ignored the rules that God had given Moses about the sacrifice.

5 The Lord was very angry with Hophni and Phinehas, Eli's sons, because they treated his sacrifices with such disrespect.

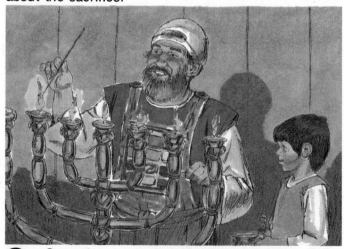

6 Samuel grew up helping Eli at the Tabernacle. He wore a special linen apron, and every year when his mother came with his father to make a sacrifice to the Lord, she brought him a new robe.

7 Eli, now an old man, kept hearing of the evil his sons were doing. He tried to make them stop, but they paid no attention to him. Therefore, the Lord decided Hophni and Phinehas must die.

8 One night Samuel was sleeping in the Tabernacle. He was awakened by a voice calling his name. He jumped up and ran to Eli to find out what the old man wanted.

9 Eli had not called him, so he sent him back to bed. This happened two more times. Finally, Eli knew the Lord was speaking to Samuel. He told the boy to say, "Speak, Lord; I am listening."

10 Samuel did so, and the Lord told him that he was going to punish Eli's wicked sons. Hophni and Phinehas would die; no sacrifice could remove the guilt of their sin.

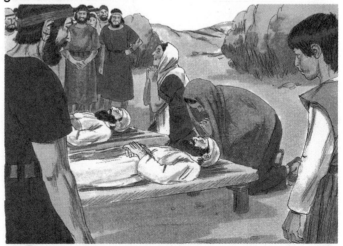

11 Samuel was afraid to tell Eli what the Lord had said. But the next morning Eli insisted that Samuel tell him everything. Afterwards Eli said, "He is the Lord; let him do what he thinks right."

12 Before long, the word of the Lord came true. Eli's wicked sons were killed in a battle with the Philistines. But the Lord was with Samuel, and everyone could see that he was a prophet.

The Israelites Demand a King

1 When Samuel grew old, he appointed his sons as judges. Unfortunately, his sons were not honest judges but were willing to take bribes.

2 Because of this, all the leaders of Israel came to Samuel and said, "Look, you are getting old, and your sons are not good men. So appoint a king to rule over us, as in other countries."

3 This request made Samuel unhappy, so he prayed about it. The Lord answered him: "It is not you they are rejecting, but me. So listen to them, but warn them clearly how their king will treat them."

4 Thus Samuel warned the people: "Your king will make your children work for him and will take your animals and land and crops for himself. But when you complain, God will not listen."

5 Yet the people paid no attention. "We want a king to rule us and lead us in war, so that we will be like other nations," they insisted.

6 After Samuel had listened to everything they had to say, he reported it to the Lord. Then the Lord said to Samuel, "Do what they want and give them a king."

7 One day some donkeys belonging to Kish, a rich man of the tribe of Benjamin, wandered off. So he said to his tall, good-looking son Saul, "Take a servant and go look for my donkeys."

8 Saul and the servant searched for a long time but could not find the donkeys. They were about to go back when the servant said, "There is a holy man in this town. Maybe he can help us."

9 Two girls at the edge of the town told them the prophet had just arrived to offer a sacrifice and hold a feast. As they entered the town, Saul and his servant met Samuel.

10 Now the day before, the Lord had said to Samuel, "Tomorrow I will send you a man from the tribe of Benjamin. Anoint him as ruler of Israel. He will rescue my people from the Philistines."

11 When Samuel saw Saul, he heard the Lord say, "This is the man who will rule over my people." Samuel told Saul that his father's donkeys had been found.

12 Then Samuel said to Saul, "Who is it that the people of Israel want so much? It is you!" Saul did not understand these words, but Samuel promised to explain everything the next morning.

Saul—Israel's First King

1 While searching for his father's stray donkeys, Saul had met the prophet Samuel. Samuel had surprising news for Saul: something special lay in store for him.

2 The next morning as Saul was leaving, Samuel poured olive oil on his head and kissed him. He said, "Saul, the Lord anoints you as the king of his people Israel."

3 Then Samuel called a meeting of all Israel at Mizpah: "The Lord says, 'I rescued you from Egypt, but you have rejected me by asking for a king. So now present yourselves before me.'"

4 So all Israel passed before the Lord by tribes and by families. From them, one man — Saul, a Benjaminite — was selected. Samuel announced, "This is the man whom the Lord has chosen!"

5 After he became king, Saul led the people of Israel in many battles against their enemies, and he was always victorious. Unfortunately, Saul also did some very foolish things.

6 One day Samuel came to Saul and said, "The Lord is going to punish the Amalekites. Go and attack them and destroy them completely — men, women, children, and even their animals."

7 So Saul attacked the Amalekites and defeated them. Although he killed all the people, he did not kill their king, Agag, nor did he kill the best of the sheep and cattle.

8 Samuel angrily went in search of Saul. When they met, Saul said, "I have done what God commanded." But Samuel replied, "Then why do I hear the sound of sheep and cattle?"

9 "Saul," said Samuel, "you are the leader of Israel! You have been anointed king by the Lord, who gave you orders to destroy these wicked people! Why, then, did you not obey him?"

10 Saul answered, "I did obey God! I went out as he told me to and killed all the Amalekites. But my men did not kill the best sheep and cattle. They brought them here to offer as a sacrifice."

11 Samuel said, "It is better to *obey* the Lord than to sacrifice even the best sheep to him. Because you have rejected the Lord's command, he has rejected you as king."

12 Saul and Samuel went on to Gilgal, where the prophet himself executed King Agag. After that Samuel never saw King Saul again, but he thought of him with great sorrow.

119

The Lord Chooses David

1 The Lord rejected Saul as king because of his disobedience. Then he said to Samuel, "Go to Bethlehem to a man named Jesse. I have chosen one of his sons to be king."

2 "How can I?" Samuel replied. "If Saul finds out, he will kill me." God said, "Take a calf and say that you have come to offer a sacrifice. Then invite Jesse and his sons to the sacrifice."

3 The leaders of Bethlehem were frightened, but Samuel reassured them by saying he had come to make a sacrifice. And as the Lord had instructed him, he invited Jesse and his sons.

4 When they arrived, Samuel was impressed by the oldest son. But the Lord said, "I do not look at how handsome he is but at his heart. This is not the one."

5 Then Jesse called his next son Abinadab and had him pass in front of Samuel. Samuel said, "The Lord has not chosen this son either."

6 Next Jesse had Shammah pass by Samuel. But the prophet said, "The Lord has not chosen this one either."

7 Jesse had seven of his sons pass before Samuel in this way. But Samuel always said, "This is not the one God has chosen." Then Samuel asked, "Are these all the sons you have?"

8 "There is still the youngest one," Jesse answered, "but he is tending the sheep." "Send for him," Samuel said. "We will wait on the sacrifice until he gets here."

9 Finally the youngest son, whose name was David, arrived. He was strong and healthy and had sparkling eyes. The Lord said to Samuel, "This is the one — anoint him!"

10 Samuel took the olive oil he had brought with him and anointed David in front of his brothers. Immediately the spirit of the Lord came upon David and was with him from that day on.

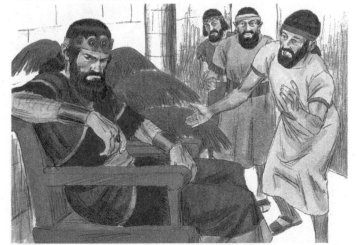

11 But the Lord's spirit had left Saul, and an evil spirit troubled him. His servants suggested he find someone to play the harp for him to cheer him up. One of them suggested David.

12 So Saul sent for David, who played his harp whenever Saul was troubled. The music always made Saul feel better. Saul was so pleased with David that he chose him as his armor-bearer.

David and Goliath

1 The Philistines again came to fight against the Israelites. The Philistines were lined up on a hill, and across a valley on another hill were the Israelite soldiers.

2 One of the Philistines was a giant named Goliath. He was over nine feet tall and wore heavy bronze armor. His spear had an iron point that weighed fifteen pounds.

3 "I challenge any one of you to fight me!" Goliath shouted. "Whoever loses, his people will be the others' slaves." Every morning and evening for forty days, the giant yelled this challenge.

4 Now Jesse was worried about his three oldest sons, who had gone off to help Saul fight the Philistines. So he sent his youngest boy, David, to find out if they were safe.

5 On arriving at the Israelite camp, David was surprised to find everyone afraid to fight the giant who challenged the army of the living God. So he said, "I will go and fight him myself."

6 But Saul said, "No, you are just a boy and he has been a soldier all his life." David replied, "I have killed lions and bears to save my father's sheep. I will do the same to this Philistine."

7 Finally Saul agreed. He gave David his own armor, but the young man was not used to it and took it off. He took his shepherd's stick, his sling, and five stones. He went to meet the giant.

8 When Goliath saw David he was filled with scorn because David was just a boy. He yelled curses at David and shouted, "I'm going to feed your body to the birds and animals!"

9 "You come with a sword and spear," David replied, "but I come in the name of the God of Israel. Today everyone will see that the Lord does not need swords or spears to save his people!"

10 Goliath started toward David. The young man ran quickly in the direction of the giant, taking a stone from his bag and slinging it. The stone struck Goliath in the forehead and broke his skull.

11 Then David ran to where Goliath had fallen to the ground and, using the giant's own sword, cut off his head!

12 Seeing their hero dead, the Philistines turned and ran. The Israelites chased the Philistines all the way back to their own country. David had won a great victory for Israel.

Saul Is Jealous

1 David had won a surprising victory over the Philistine giant, Goliath. As he returned home, women from all the towns of Israel came out to meet him and sing his praises.

2 King Saul became angry when he heard them praising David. He thought to himself, "They are praising him more than me. Next they will want to make David a king." Saul was very jealous.

3 But Jonathan, Saul's son, loved David very much. Jonathan promised David that he would be his friend forever. He even gave David his robe and sword and other weapons.

4 One day as King Saul listened to David play his harp, an evil spirit took control of the king. He tried to kill David with his spear. However, David jumped out of the way and was not hurt.

5 Later Saul made David commander in the army, hoping he would be killed in battle. But David was a good leader, because the Lord was with him. Everyone but Saul liked David.

6 Then Michal, one of Saul's daughters, fell in love with David. Saul was glad to hear this, because he thought it would give him a chance to get rid of David.

7 Saul told David he could marry Michal if he killed 100 Philistines. He hoped David would be killed. But David succeeded in killing 200 Philistines! Saul had to let David marry Michal.

8 Saul had promised Jonathan that he would not harm David. But one day as Saul listened to David play the harp, an evil spirit again caused him to try to kill David. David got away unhurt.

9 That night Saul sent some men to watch David's house, with orders to kill him in the morning. Michal knew David was in danger, and she warned him that he must escape that very night.

10 Michal helped David climb down from the window and escape. Then she put the household gods in David's bed and covered them up so that it looked as though David were still asleep.

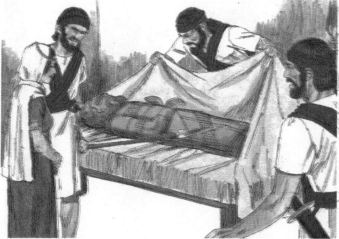

11 When Saul's men came for David the next morning, Michal told them her husband was sick and in bed. By the time these men discovered that they had been tricked, David had gotten away.

12 David fled to Ramah, where Samuel the prophet lived. David planned to live with Samuel for a while. But before long, Saul found out where David was and sent his men to capture him.

David and Jonathan

1 Fearing for his life, David escaped from King Saul's men and fled to Ramah, where the prophet Samuel lived. But Saul soon learned where he was, so David went to Jonathan to ask for help.

2 At first Jonathan couldn't believe his father would break his promise not to hurt David. Finally David convinced him. Then they made a plan, for David was to eat with Saul the next day.

3 At the feast, Saul sat in his usual place, with Jonathan opposite him. David's place was empty. (He was hiding in a field waiting for Jonathan.) Saul said nothing about David that night.

4 Again the next night, David did not come to the feast. So Saul said to Jonathan, "Why did David not eat with us yesterday and today?"

5 Jonathan replied, "David asked permission to go to Bethlehem. His family is offering a sacrifice, and his brother wanted him to come home for it. So I said he could go."

6 Saul was furious. "Your friendship with David is a disgrace!" he shouted. "Don't you know that as long as David is alive, you can never become king yourself? David must die!"

7 "But why should David die?" Jonathan asked. "What has he done?" In anger Saul threw his spear at his own son. Now Jonathan knew that his father did indeed intend to kill David.

8 The next day Jonathan went to the field where David was hiding. He shot some arrows beyond where his servant was standing and yelled, "They're past you. Hurry and bring them here."

9 The boy did not know, of course, that this was Jonathan's signal to David that he must go away. Jonathan then gave his bow and arrows to the boy and told him to take them back to town.

10 When the boy had gone, David came out of hiding and fell on his knees before Jonathan, bowing with his face to the ground three times.

11 Jonathan and David were very sad. They cried as they kissed each other goodbye. David cried even harder than Jonathan.

12 Jonathan said, "God be with you, David. You and I, and our children, too, will always keep the promise of friendship we have made." So David left Jonathan and went away to hide from Saul.

Saul Chases David

1 After leaving Jonathan, David and his men hid at different places in the wilderness west of the Dead Sea. Word reached them that the town of Keilah, north of Hebron, was being attacked by Philistines.

2 David asked the Lord whether he should try to save the town, and the answer was yes. So he and his men attacked the Philistines and defeated them, just as the Lord had promised.

3 Hearing that David was at Keilah, Saul set out to capture him. David and his men fled when the Lord warned them that the people would turn them over to Saul. So Saul had to give up his plan.

4 Then one day some people from Ziph came to Saul and told him that David was hiding near their town. Saul said, "Find out exactly where he is, and I will go capture him." Then he sent them back.

5 Soon afterwards, Saul led his men to Ziph. He almost caught up with David there. Saul's men were on one side of a mountain and David's were on the other, trying to get away.

6 Just then, a messenger arrived and said to Saul, "You must come home at once! The Philistines are attacking our country!" Immediately Saul returned home, allowing David to escape.

7 After the Philistine threat, Saul heard that David was hiding near Engedi. He took 3,000 men and began a new search for David. One day he saw a cave near some sheep pens beside the road.

8 Saul went into the cave alone for a minute. It happened that David and his men were hiding in the darkness in that very cave! David's men urged him to kill Saul. "This is your chance," they said.

9 But David did not harm Saul. Instead he slipped up close to the king in the darkness and cut off a piece of his robe. Saul did not know that anything at all had happened.

10 As Saul left the cave, David followed him and called out to him, "Saul, I could have killed you just now, as this piece I cut from your robe proves. I do not want to harm you! Why are you trying to kill me?"

11 Saul said, "Is it really you, David?" He began to cry. "You are right and I am wrong," he said. "You have shown your goodness to me by not killing me when you had the chance."

12 "Now I am sure you will be the king of Israel," Saul said. "Just promise me that you will not kill my descendants." David promised, and Saul returned home. David and his men remained in a safe place.

The Last Days of Saul

1 Samuel the prophet died in his old age and was buried in his hometown, Ramah. Some time after that, the Philistines again made war on Israel.

2 The Philistines brought their army to a place near Shunem. Saul and his soldiers went out to defend their country. They camped on Mount Gilboa. But when Saul saw the Philistine army, he was afraid.

3 Saul tried to find out what the Lord wanted him to do. But the Lord gave Saul no answer. So Saul decided to visit a medium (a person who claims he can speak to the spirits of the dead).

4 Now Saul had already outlawed all mediums from the land of Israel. But his servants knew that there was a woman living at Endor who was a medium. Saul put on a disguise and went to see her.

5 He said to her, "Speak to the spirits and call up the one I tell you." But the woman was suspicious, fearing it was a trap. "Surely you know that King Saul has forbidden anyone to do that," she said.

6 Saul promised her she would be safe. Then he asked her to call back the spirit of the prophet Samuel. When Saul heard Samuel's voice, he said, "I am in great trouble, Samuel. Tell me what I must do,"

7 Samuel replied, "Because you have disobeyed the Lord, he is giving your kingdom to David. The Philistines will defeat you, and tomorrow you and your sons will be with me." Saul was terrified.

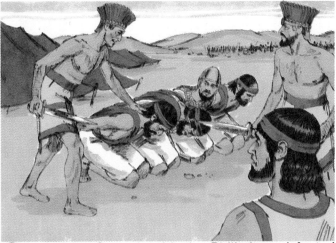

8 Just as Samuel said, the Philistines defeated the Israelites the next day. Many Israelites were killed, and the rest fled. The enemy captured Saul's sons, including Jonathan, and killed them.

9 Saul had been badly wounded by an arrow. Not wanting to be captured, he asked his armor bearer to kill him. But the armor bearer would not do that. So Saul killed himself by falling on his own sword.

10 The next day the Philistines found the bodies of Saul and his sons. They cut off Saul's head, and they nailed his body and his sons' bodies to the wall of the city of Beth-shan.

11 When the Israelites who lived in Jabesh heard about this, some of their bravest men went to Beth-shan and took down the bodies. They buried Saul and his sons near a great tree in Jabesh.

12 After David mourned Saul and Jonathan, he moved to Hebron. The people of Judah came to him there and anointed him their king. Later he was anointed as king over the remainder of Israel.

King David Shows Kindness

1 King David ruled over all of Israel and made sure that his people were always treated fairly and justly.

2 One day David asked, "Is there anyone from Saul's family still living? If so, I would like to show him kindness for Jonathan's sake."

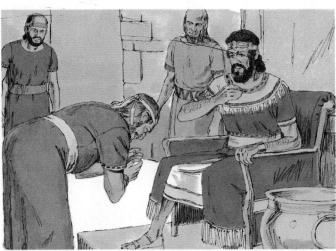

3 A man who had been one of Saul's servants said to David, "Jonathan's son Mephibosheth is still alive. But he is unable to walk, because both his feet were hurt when he was just five years old."

4 David then called Mephibosheth to him. "Don't be afraid," David said. "I will show you kindness because your father was my friend. I will give you all the land that once belonged to your grandfather Saul."

5 The king said to the man who had been Saul's servant, "Take care of Mephibosheth's land for him. He will always be a guest at my table." So Mephibosheth became like one of David's own sons.

6 But not all of David's efforts to be kind turned out so well. When the king of Ammon died, David said to his servants, "I will show friendship to the king's son just as the king did to me."

7 So he sent messengers to express his sympathy to the king's son. But the leaders said to the king's son, "David did not send these messengers to express sympathy! They have come to spy on us!"

8 So the king's son had the messengers' beards shaved off on one side and their clothes cut off at the waist. Then he sent them away. They were too embarrassed to return until their beards grew out.

9 The Ammonites knew that their actions had made David their enemy. So they hired 33,000 soldiers from Syria and other places to come help them fight against King David.

10 The Israelite soldiers fought in two groups, one against the Syrians and one against the Ammonites. When they started toward the Syrians, the Syrians ran away. Then the Ammonites also fled.

11 After this defeat, the Syrians called for all their troops in other places to come back and help. This time King David himself led the Israelites. They killed 700 chariot drivers and 40,000 horsemen.

12 Even the Syrian commander was killed. Afterwards the kings who had helped the Syrians made peace with Israel. The Syrians were afraid to help the Ammonites fight Israel after this defeat.

133

David and Bathsheba

1 During the spring one year, King David sent Joab and the Israelite army off to fight against the Ammonites at Rabbah. But David himself stayed in Jerusalem.

2 One day after waking from his afternoon nap, David went up to the palace roof to take a walk. From the roof he saw a very beautiful woman bathing. She was Bathsheba, wife of Uriah the Hittite.

3 At that time Uriah was away fighting at Rabbah. David had Bathsheba brought to the palace as if she were his wife. Later Bathsheba sent word to David that she was going to have a baby.

4 At first David tried to get Uriah to go home so that Uriah would think the baby was his own. When that didn't work, David had Uriah put in a dangerous position during a battle, and he was killed.

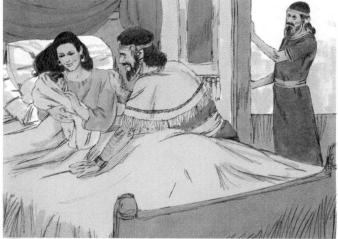

5 After Uriah's death, David made Bathsheba his wife. In a few months, she gave birth to a baby boy. But the Lord was not pleased with David. He sent Nathan the prophet to tell the king this story:

6 "A rich man and a poor man lived in the same town. The rich man had many sheep, but the poor man had only one little lamb. The poor man loved it like one of his own children."

7 "Then one day a visitor came to see the rich man. The rich man didn't want to kill one of his own sheep to feed his guest. So he took the poor man's pet lamb and cooked it for his visitor to eat."

8 David became angry. "That man ought to die!" he said. Nathan replied, "You are that man! The Lord says, 'I have done so much for you. Why have you done this evil — killing Uriah and taking his wife?' "

9 Then David was sorry for his wrong. "I have sinned," he cried. Nathan said, "The Lord forgives you, and you will not die. But because you have shown such contempt for the Lord, your child will die."

10 The baby, indeed, became very sick. David prayed that his child would get well. David would not eat anything, and he lay on the floor all night long. No one could comfort him.

11 After about a week, David's little son died. The servants were afraid to tell David. When they did, he washed himself and went to worship the Lord. Then he went home and comforted Bathsheba.

12 Later David and Bathsheba had another baby, also a boy. David named him Solomon. The Lord loved Solomon very much. Solomon would grow up to be a very wise and wealthy man.

The Songs of David

1 David, the king of Israel, had played the harp from the time he was just a boy. He was skilled at writing songs of praise, called "psalms." These were poems which were put to music.

2 In his songs, David spoke of God's greatness: *Your greatness is seen in all the world! Your praise reaches up to the heavens; it is sung by children and babies.*

3 When he was young, David had cared for sheep. He knew that God would care for him that way: *The Lord is my shepherd: I have everything I need.*

4 *Even if I go through the deepest darkness, I will not be afraid, Lord, for you are with me. Your shepherd's rod and staff protect me.*

5 Some psalms are prayers for forgiveness: *Be merciful, O God, because of your love. Because of your great mercy wipe away my sins! Wash away all my evil and make me clean from my sin!*

6 *Create a pure heart in me, O God . . . Give me again the joy that comes from your salvation . . . Then I will teach sinners your commands, and they will turn back to you.*

7 Other psalms are prayers for aid or rescue: *I am weak and helpless; come to me quickly, O God. You are my savior and my Lord!*

8 David often sang of his gratitude to God: *I praise the Lord, because he guides me, and in the night my conscience warns me. I am always aware of the Lord's presence.*

9 You, Lord, are all I have, and you give me all I need; my future is in your hands. How wonderful are your gifts to me!

10 He sang of the joy that comes from obeying God: *Happy are those whose lives are faultless, who live according to the Law of the Lord. Happy are those who follow his commands.*

11 I delight in following your commands more than in having great wealth. I take pleasure in your laws; your commands I will not forget.

12 David's songs expressed great love for God: *I will praise you, Lord, with all my heart; I will tell of all the wonderful things you have done. I will sing with joy because of you.*

Solomon Becomes King

1 King David had many problems with his sons that caused him great sadness. Once his son Absalom tried to take over as king. David wept when Absalom was killed by the commander of David's army.

2 Now David was old and had to stay in bed. His son Adonijah wanted very much to be king. He got himself a chariot and horses and an escort of fifty men.

3 Adonijah also got the army commander Joab and the priest Abiathar to promise to help him. Then Adonijah held a feast. He invited all the sons of David except Solomon, whose mother was Bathsheba.

4 Hearing this, Nathan the prophet went to Bathsheba to warn her. "Adonijah has made himself king!" he said. "If you want to save yourself and Solomon, you'd better tell David at once."

5 So Bathsheba went to the king's room and told him what Adonijah had done. David said, "Today I will keep my promise to you that your son Solomon would be the next king."

6 David gave instructions to Zadok the priest and Nathan the prophet. They had Solomon ride on David's own mule to the Gihon spring. There they anointed Solomon, making him king of Israel.

7 They blew a trumpet, and all the people shouted, "Long live King Solomon!" The people followed Solomon back to the city, shouting and playing on flutes and making a great noise.

8 Adonijah and the king's sons were finishing the feast when they heard this noise. Soon a messenger arrived and said, "David has made Solomon king!" They were all afraid and left for their homes.

9 Adonijah was also afraid of Solomon. He fled to the altar of burnt offering and put his hands on one of its corners. He thought he would be safe there, because the Law of Moses would protect him.

10 Solomon sent for Adonijah, who came and bowed low before him. In this way Adonijah admitted that Solomon was the rightful king. Solomon then let him go home without punishing him.

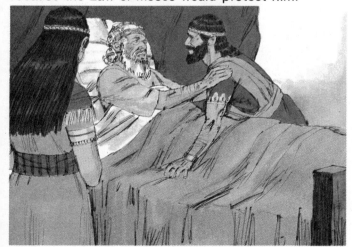

11 Later, David said to Solomon, "I am about to die. Be sure to obey all the commandments of the Law of Moses. Then the Lord will keep his promise that my descendants will always rule over Israel."

12 So David died and was buried in Jerusalem. He had been king for forty years. His son Solomon, the new king, grew stronger all the time and gained complete control over the land.

The Wisdom of Solomon

1 One day King Solomon went to Gibeon to offer sacrifices at the famous altar there. He had gone there many times before, but this time something different happened.

2 As Solomon slept that night, he had a dream. In the dream, the Lord appeared to him and asked, "Solomon, what would you like me to give you?"

3 Solomon replied, "O Lord, you have made me king after my father, but I am still young. I do not know how to be a king. Give me the wisdom to rule your people in the right way."

4 The Lord was pleased that Solomon's request was not a selfish one. "I will do what you have asked," God said. "I will give you more wisdom than anyone else in the world."

5 "I will also give you what you did not ask for: you will have more wealth and honor than any other king! And if you keep my laws, as your father David did, I will give you a long life."

6 When Solomon woke up, he realized that God had spoken to him through a dream. When he returned to Jerusalem, he offered sacrifices to God and gave a feast for his officials.

7 One day two women came to King Solomon. They wanted him to settle a dispute. One of them said, "Sir, this woman and I live in the same house, and both of us have given birth to baby boys."

8 "During the night she accidentally killed her baby by rolling over on it. Then she took my baby and put the dead baby in my bed. When I woke up, I found the dead baby — but it was not mine!"

9 The other woman spoke up. "No!" she said. "The living child is mine! The dead one is yours!"

10 Then King Solomon sent his servant for a sword. When it was brought, he ordered the servant, "Cut the child in two and give each of the women half of it."

11 The mother cried, "Oh, no! Don't kill the child! Give it to her!" The other woman said, "Go ahead and cut it in two." Then Solomon said, "Stop! Give it to the first woman — she's the real mother."

12 The people of Israel were filled with respect for Solomon when they heard of his decision. They understood that God had given him special wisdom.

Solomon Builds the Temple

1 While David was king, there were many wars. But when Solomon became king, there was peace in the land. So Solomon decided to build a temple for the Lord, as the Lord promised he could.

2 Solomon arranged for King Hiram of Tyre to cut down great cedar trees and float them along the seacoast to Israel. He sent thousands of Israelites to help cut the trees. Many others cut out huge stones.

3 It took seven years to complete the Temple. In the courtyard were a bronze altar and a huge tank of water resting on the backs of twelve bronze bulls. A tall pillar stood on each side of the doorway.

4 Inside, the walls of the two main rooms were covered with carved cedar overlaid with gold. In the larger room, the Holy Place, were ten lampstands, an altar, and a table — all of gold.

5 The smaller room, the Most Holy Place, was a perfect cube. In it were two large winged creatures made of olive wood and covered with gold.

6 When the temple was finished, all the leaders of Israel gathered in Jerusalem. The priests carried the sacred Covenant Box into the temple and placed it in the Most Holy Place.

7 The Levites and priests next carried in all the new equipment — golden tables, lamps, dishes, and utensils. They also stored the old Tabernacle, which Moses had built, in the new Temple.

8 As the priests left the Temple, it was suddenly filled with a cloud. This was a sign that the Lord was present. Thousands of animals were offered as sacrifices to the Lord that day.

9 King Solomon prayed: "Lord God of Israel, there is no God like you in heaven or earth. Please keep your promise that one of my father David's descendants will always rule over Israel."

10 "Watch over this Temple day and night," he prayed. "And hear your people when we face in the direction of this Temple and pray. In your home in heaven hear us and forgive us."

11 The Lord answered Solomon, saying, "This Temple will be the place where I shall be worshiped forever. I will watch over it and protect it. And I will let your descendants rule over Israel."

12 "But if you or your descendants disobey me and worship other gods, I will move my people Israel from this land and depart from this Temple. I will leave it in a heap of ruins."

Solomon Disobeys God

1 God blessed King Solomon with great wealth and wisdom. But Solomon married many foreign women, even though the Lord had warned him not to.

2 Solomon had married 700 princesses, and he had 300 concubines. He built places around Jerusalem where his wives could burn incense and make sacrifices to the gods of their own countries.

3 By the time he was old, Solomon himself was unfaithful to the Lord. He, too, worshiped Astoreth, the goddess of Sidon, and Milcom, the god of Ammon, and others.

4 God was angry with Solomon. "You have not obeyed me," said the Lord. "Therefore, I am going to take the kingdom away from you and give it to someone else."

5 Later Solomon had some repairs made on the walls of Jerusalem. As he watched the workmen, he noticed a man named Jeroboam. Solomon put Jeroboam in charge of the other workers.

6 One day Jeroboam happened to meet a prophet named Ahijah on a country road. Ahijah stopped him, took off his robe, and tore it into twelve pieces.

7 "Take any ten pieces you wish," Ahijah said, "for the Lord is going to take away the kingdom from Solomon. He will give you ten of the tribes to rule over."

8 "The Lord says, 'For the sake of my servant David, I will not do this during Solomon's lifetime. I will leave Solomon's son one tribe to rule, because of my promise to David, who was loyal to me.' "

9 Ahijah continued: "The Lord says, 'I am doing this because Solomon rejected me and worshiped other gods. But if you obey me, I will be with you and make your descendants kings after you.' "

10 Somehow Solomon found out what Ahijah had told Jeroboam, and he tried to kill Jeroboam. However, Jeroboam managed to escape and went to Egypt. He lived there until Solomon died.

11 Solomon ruled as king of Israel in Jerusalem for forty years. When he died, he was buried in the city of David. His son Rehoboam became king after him.

12 News of Solomon's death reached Jeroboam in Egypt. He thought he would be safe now, so he returned to the land of Israel. Thus was the stage set for God to carry out his plan.

The Kingdom Is Divided

1 After Solomon died, his son Rehoboam became king. Jeroboam, who had fled from Solomon, returned from Egypt to Israel. Now the crowning of Rehoboam as king was to take place at Shechem.

2 But at Shechem the northern tribes complained to Rehoboam. They said, "Your father treated us badly and made life hard for us. If you will make life easier for us, we will always be your loyal subjects."

3 Rehoboam ignored the wise advice of his older advisers. His reply to the leaders of the northern tribes was rude and harsh. "I am going to make life even harder for you than my father did!" he said.

4 In anger they shouted, "We will have nothing more to do with David and his family!" So they made Jeroboam their king. Only the tribe of Judah remained loyal to David's descendant, Rehoboam.

5 The Temple of the Lord was in Jerusalem, which is in Judah. So Jeroboam thought, "If my people continue to go to Jerusalem to worship, they will again become loyal to David's descendant, King Rehoboam."

6 So Jeroboam made two calves of gold, putting one at Bethel and the other at Dan. He said to the people, "Don't go to Jerusalem any more. These are your gods! Worship them at Dan and Bethel."

7 God was not pleased with Jeroboam. He sent a prophet to Bethel to say, "Someday a child will be born in the family of David who will kill on this altar all the priests who serve pagan gods."

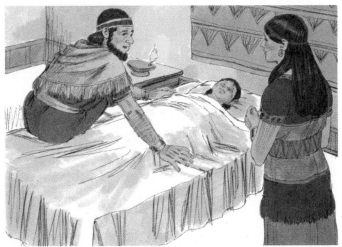

8 Some time later, King Jeroboam's son became ill. Jeroboam said to his wife, "Put on a disguise and go to Shiloh. Ask Ahijah the prophet what will happen to our son."

9 But the Lord revealed to Ahijah who she was. Ahijah said to her, "Tell Jeroboam that God took the kingdom from David's descendants and gave it to him because David's descendants had sinned."

10 "But Jeroboam has sinned even more than they did! Therefore, God will destroy all his male descendants! Now go home. When you get there, your son will die." It happened just as Ahijah said.

11 The people of Judah also sinned against the Lord. They built places of worship for false gods and set up stone pillars for worship on the hills, just as the Canaanites had once done.

12 Several years later, the Egyptians attacked Jerusalem. They took away all the treasures of the Temple and of the palace. Because the Israelites had sinned, the Lord did not protect them or the Temple.

Elijah and the Widow

1 Many years had passed since the Israelites divided into two kingdoms, Israel in the north and Judah in the south. A man named Ahab was now king of Israel. His capital was the city of Samaria.

2 Ahab was more evil than any king before him. He married a foreign woman named Jezebel and worshiped her gods. He built a temple for Baal in Samaria and set up an image of the goddess Asherah.

3 Then a prophet named Elijah came to King Ahab and said, "In the name of the Lord I tell you that there will be no dew or rain during the next few years unless I say so."

4 God told Elijah to go to the brook Cherith. There, just as God had promised, the ravens brought him food every morning and evening. But soon the brook dried up, for there had been no rain.

5 So God said to Elijah, "Go to the town of Zarephath, near Sidon, and stay there. I have commanded a widow who lives there to feed you."

6 When Elijah got to Zarephath, he saw a widow gathering firewood near the town gate. He asked her for a drink of water and some bread.

7 She replied, "I'm sorry, but we don't have any bread. I have only a handful of flour and a little olive oil. After I cook that for my son and myself, we will die."

8 "Go ahead," Elijah said, "but first bake a small loaf for me. God has promised that you will not run out of food before he sends rain again." Indeed, there was enough for the three of them for a long time.

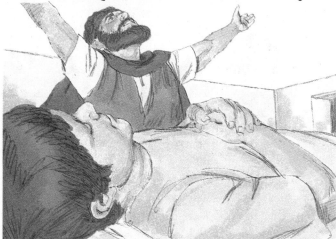

9 Some time passed. The widow's son became very sick. He grew worse and worse until he died. The woman was very unhappy with Elijah and blamed him for her child's death.

10 Elijah carried the boy upstairs to the bed. Then he prayed aloud: "O Lord, why have you done such a terrible thing to this poor widow? She has been kind to me but you have caused her son to die!"

11 Then Elijah stretched himself out on the boy three times and prayed, "O Lord, please restore this child to life!"

12 The Lord answered Elijah's prayer and caused the child to breathe again! Elijah took him down to his mother. She said, "Now I know that you really are a prophet through whom the Lord speaks."

Elijah on Mount Carmel

1 There had been no rain for about three years. The famine was very bad in Samaria. Jezebel, the queen of Israel, was killing the prophets of the Lord. Then God sent Elijah to see King Ahab again.

2 When they met, Ahab said, "There you are, you troublemaker!" Elijah replied, "You are the troublemaker. You are the one disobeying the Lord by worshiping Baal!"

3 Elijah said, "Order all your people to meet me at Mount Carmel. And bring the 450 prophets of Baal and the 400 prophets of the goddess Asherah whom Jezebel supports."

4 When everyone had gathered on Mount Carmel, Elijah said, "How long will it take you to make up your minds? If the Lord is God, follow him; but if Baal is God, follow him!" No one answered.

5 Then Elijah said, "Let the prophets of Baal prepare a sacrifice and place it on the wood — without lighting the fire. Then I will do the same. The god who answers our prayers with fire—he is God."

6 The prophets of Baal prayed until noon. They danced around the altar they had built, shouting, "Answer us, O Baal!" But no answer came.

7 Elijah began to make fun of them. "Pray louder!" he said. "Maybe your god is asleep or away on a trip!" They danced and shouted till the middle of the afternoon. Still there was no answer.

8 Then Elijah prepared an altar for the Lord and put his sacrifice on it. He dug a trench around the base and had water poured over the sacrifice and wood until it ran down and filled up the trench.

9 Elijah prayed, "O Lord, God of Abraham, Isaac, and Jacob, prove now that you are the God of Israel and that I am your servant!"

10 And the Lord answered with fire! The fire burned up the sacrifice, the wood, the stones, and the soil around the altar! It even dried up the water in the trench around the altar!

11 When the people saw this, they fell to the ground, shouting, "The Lord is God; he alone is God!" Then Elijah took all the prophets of Baal to the brook called Kishon and there he killed them.

12 Afterward, Elijah said to Ahab, "Go home, for soon it will rain." As Elijah waited on the mountain, the sky grew dark, the wind blew, and heavy rain began to fall. The long drought was over.

Elijah in the Whirlwind

1 One day Elijah, the prophet, and his friend Elisha were walking together. Suddenly Elijah said, "Stay here. The Lord has told me to go to Bethel." But Elisha insisted on going with him.

2 A group of prophets lived at Bethel. They said to Elisha, "Do you know that the Lord is going to take away your master from you today?" Elisha said, "Yes, I know, but do not talk about it."

3 Then Elijah said to Elisha, "Stay here. The Lord has sent me to Jericho." But Elisha said, "As surely as the Lord is living, I will not leave you." So they went on to Jericho together.

4 Again at Jericho, the prophets who lived there came to Elisha and said, "Do you know that the Lord is going to take your master from you today?" Elisha answered, "Yes, but do not talk about it."

5 "Stay here," Elijah said. "The Lord has told me to go to the Jordan River." But Elisha said, "I will not leave you!" So they went on, followed by fifty prophets.

6 As the fifty prophets watched, Elijah took off his cloak and hit the water with it. The water divided! Elijah and Elisha walked across on dry ground!

7 On the other side of the Jordan, Elijah asked Elisha, "What shall I do for you before I am taken away?" Elisha answered, "Please give me a double share of your spirit."

8 "That is very difficult," said Elijah, "but if you see me as I am being taken away, you will receive it. If you do not see me being taken away, you will not receive it."

9 As they walked together, talking, a chariot of fire pulled by horses of fire suddenly came between them. Elijah was taken up into heaven by a whirlwind!

10 Elisha was watching and saw this happen. He cried out, "My father, my father! The chariots and horsemen of Israel!" He was very sad and tore his clothing into pieces. He never saw Elijah again.

11 Then Elisha picked up the cloak that Elijah had dropped and struck the Jordan just as Elijah had done. Elisha said, "Where is the Lord, the God of Elijah?" The water parted and he crossed over.

12 The fifty prophets who had been watching from a distance said to each other, "The spirit of Elijah is resting on Elisha." Then they went to meet him and bowed to the ground before him.

Naaman the Leper

1 In the days of the prophet Elisha, the commander of the army of Syria—one of the countries next to Israel—was a man whose name was Naaman.

2 Naaman was very famous in Syria. He was a great soldier; he and his army had won many victories. But there was something wrong with Naaman. He had a terrible skin disease called leprosy.

3 Now, a little Israelite girl who had been captured by the Syrians lived in Naaman's house. She said to Naaman's wife, "I wish my master could go to Israel. There's a prophet there who could cure him."

4 So Naaman got permission from the king of Syria to go to Israel. He took a gift of silver and gold and fine clothing. The king also gave him a letter which ordered the king of Israel to heal Naaman.

5 The king of Israel was very upset when he read this letter. "How can he expect me to cure this man?" he said. "Who does he think I am— God? He must be trying to start a fight."

6 Elisha the prophet found out about Naaman and the letter. He said to the king of Israel: "Send the man to me. I will show him that there is a prophet in Israel."

7 So Naaman went to Elisha's house. Elisha's servant came out and said to Naaman, "My master says you are to wash yourself in the Jordan river seven times. Then you will be cured of your disease."

8 When Naaman heard this, he became very angry. "We have better rivers back in Syria! I thought the prophet would do something special, like praying for me or waving his hand over my leprosy!"

9 But his servants said to him, "Sir, if this prophet had told you to do something difficult, you would have done it, wouldn't you? So why don't you just wash yourself as he said?"

10 Then Naaman went to the Jordan and dipped himself in it seven times, as Elisha had instructed. When he finished, his disease was healed! His skin was just as healthy as a child's!

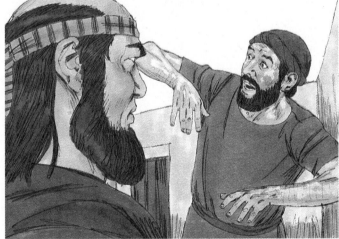

11 He went back to Elisha and said, "Now I know that there is no god but the God of Israel." He tried to get Elisha to accept a gift, but no matter how hard he persuaded, Elisha would not take it.

12 After Naaman left, Elisha's servant followed him and asked for a gift. Later Elisha scolded the servant and said, "You will get Naaman's disease." And the servant's skin became white with leprosy.

Joash the Boy King

1 Both Judah and Israel had many evil kings. When King Ahaziah of Judah died, his mother Athaliah wanted to be queen. She had all her grandsons killed so none of them could be king.

2 Only Joash, a one-year-old child, escaped. His aunt, Jehosheba, the wife of Jehoiada the priest, saved him. She kept him hidden in one of the rooms of the Temple for six years.

3 When Joash was seven, Jehoiada carried out a plan to make Joash king. Protected by soldiers, Jehoiada crowned Joash and anointed his head with oil. The people shouted, "Long live the king!"

4 Hearing the noise, Athaliah hurried to the Temple. When she saw Joash, she tore her clothes and cried, "Treason!" Some soldiers were ordered to take her out of the Temple and kill her.

5 Jehoiada the priest had the boy king Joash and the people of Judah make a covenant with the Lord. They promised again that they would be the Lord's people.

6 Then the people went to the temple of Baal and tore it down. They destroyed the altars and broke the idols into pieces. They killed the priest of Baal in front of the altars.

7 After several years, Joash decided to repair the Lord's Temple. He ordered the priests to collect money for making the repairs. But many years passed and still no repairs were made.

8 Finally Joash decided he must do something. He had a large box placed by the Temple gate. When the people came to offer sacrifices, they could put their money gift for the Temple in the box.

9 This money was used to pay the carpenters and stonemasons and metal workers who made the repairs on the Temple. Before long, the Temple was strong and beautiful as before.

10 As long as Jehoiada the priest was alive, sacrifices were made at the Temple every day. But when he died, the people stopped coming there. They began worshiping images of the goddess Asherah.

11 The Lord sent Zechariah, the son of Jehoiada, to warn Joash. He said: "Because you have forsaken the Lord, he has forsaken you." Joash was angry and ordered Zechariah to be stoned to death.

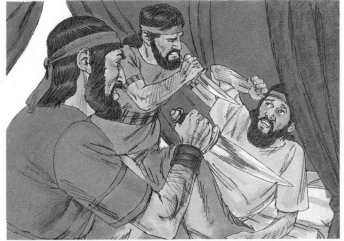

12 Later that year, the Syrian army attacked Judah and Jerusalem. King Joash was wounded during the battle. While still in bed, he was murdered by two men who had been friends of Zechariah.

The End of Israel

1 A few of the kings of Judah were good men, loyal to the Lord. But all of the kings of Israel, the northern kingdom, were men who did evil in the sight of the Lord.

2 Menahem, for example, became king of Israel by killing King Shallum—who had killed the king before him. Menahem was king for ten years but he did nothing to turn his people from their sins.

3 While Menahem was ruler, Tiglath-Pilesar of Assyria led his army against Israel. In order to remain king of Israel, Menahem had to give Tiglath-Pilesar a huge amount of silver.

4 When Menahem died, his son Pekahiah became king. After ruling for only two years, Pekahiah was murdered by Pekah, who became the next king.

5 During the time of Pekah, Tiglath-Pilesar brought his army to Israel again. He captured many cities in Galilee and Gilead and took many people to Assyria as prisoners.

6 After that, Pekah was killed by Hoshea, who then became king. During his reign, the new king of Assyria, Shalmaneser, attacked Israel.

7 Hoshea paid Shalmaneser a great amount of money each year in order to remain king. Finally, Hoshea decided he would pay no more. Then Shalmaneser and the Assyrian army attacked Israel.

8 The Assyrians besieged the city of Samaria for three years before it surrendered. Then the king of Assyria took all the people of Israel back to the land of Assyria, where he forced them to live.

9 The king of Assyria made people from Babylonia and Elam and Syria move to Israel and live in the cities that had once been the home of the Israelites.

10 Israel was not destroyed because the Lord was unable to protect his people. Rather, Israel was destroyed because the people had sinned against the Lord by worshiping other gods.

11 The Lord had sent his messengers—the prophets—to warn Israel by saying, "Give up your evil ways and obey the Lord." But the people had ignored the prophets.

12 The people of Israel did not keep the covenant their ancestors had made with the Lord. So the Lord removed them from the land he had given them. Only the tribe of Judah was left.

The Story of Jonah

1 In the days when Assyria was still a great nation, the Lord called a prophet named Jonah. He said, "Go to the city of Nineveh, the capital of Assyria, and preach against it, for it is very wicked."

2 Jonah, however, did not want to preach to the people of Nineveh, because the Assyrians were enemies of Israel. So Jonah got on a ship going in the opposite direction from Nineveh.

3 As the ship sailed, a terrible storm came up. The wind was so strong that the ship was about to sink. The frightened sailors threw all the cargo overboard to keep it afloat.

4 But the storm continued to get worse. Finally, Jonah said to the sailors, "This storm is all my fault, because I have run away from the Lord. Throw me into the sea, and it will calm down."

5 The sailors didn't want to hurt Jonah. But there was nothing else they could do. They threw Jonah into the stormy sea. Immediately the sea became calm! The sailors were amazed and frightened.

6 Jonah did not drown in the sea, for the Lord prepared a great fish to swallow him. Three days later, the fish spit Jonah up onto the land.

7 The Lord now spoke to Jonah a second time, saying, "Go and preach to the people of Nineveh." This time Jonah obeyed. He went straight to Nineveh and preached.

8 The message of the Lord was simple: "In forty days the city of Nineveh will be destroyed." The people of the city believed Jonah. All of them, even the king, repented and prayed to the Lord.

9 Therefore the Lord had mercy on them: he decided not to destroy them. This made Jonah very angry. "I knew you would forgive them!" he said. "That's why I didn't want to preach to them!"

10 Then Jonah went out to a hill near the city and built a little shelter. He sat there waiting to see what would happen. That night a vine grew up. It helped shade Jonah from the sun the next day.

11 But the day after that the vine died. As the hot east wind blew on Jonah, he said, "I wish I were dead." So God said, "Are you right to be so angry about this vine?" Jonah answered, "Yes!"

12 Then God said, "Jonah, you care so much about this vine, which you didn't even plant or work to make grow. Don't you think I should care what happens to this great city?"

Josiah Renews the Covenant

1 Many years had passed since the Assyrians destroyed the northern kingdom, Israel. When King Amon of Judah was killed, the people made his son Josiah king. Josiah was just eight years old.

2 After he had been king for many years, Josiah decided to repair the Temple. He sent his secretary Shaphan to tell the high priest to give the money collected by the priests to the Temple workers.

3 After Shaphan had given Hilkiah the high priest those orders, the high priest showed him a book which he had found in the Temple. It was the book of the laws of God's covenant with the Israelites.

4 So Shaphan reported to Josiah about the money for the repairs. Then he said, "This is a book that Hilkiah gave me." As he read it, Josiah tore his clothes in grief.

5 Josiah sent word to Huldah the prophetess about what had happened. She replied, "The Lord fully intends to destroy Jerusalem. But he will not do so while Josiah is alive."

6 Josiah ordered all the people of Judah to meet at the Temple. He read aloud to them the book that Hilkiah had found. Then he and all the people made a promise that they would obey the Lord.

7 Josiah had the priests clean out the Temple. They removed all the things that had been used to worship Baal and Asherah and the stars. Josiah burned all these things outside the city walls.

8 Josiah ruined the altar that King Solomon had built near Jerusalem for the gods of his wives. He broke the stone pillars and cut down the symbol of the goddess Asherah.

9 Throughout the land of Judah, Josiah removed the priests who had made sacrifices to other gods. He destroyed the place where they had burned their children as offerings to the god Milcom.

10 Josiah destroyed the place of worship at Bethel which Jeroboam had built when the kingdom was first divided. Then he went through the towns of Israel and tore down all the altars.

11 Finally Josiah ordered the people to celebrate the Passover. No Passover had been celebrated like that by any of the kings of Judah or Israel since the time of the judges.

12 No other king turned to the Lord as Josiah did. He obeyed the law of God with all his soul and all his strength.

The Fall of Jerusalem

1 When Jehoiachin became king at the age of eighteen, the kingdom of Judah was in great danger. His father Jehoiakim had rebelled against Babylon. For a while Babylon did nothing about it.

2 But soon after Jehoiachin became king, Nebuchadnezzar of Babylon attacked Jerusalem. Jehoiachin had been king only three months when he had to surrender.

3 Nebuchadnezzar took Jehoiachin, his mother and wives, and many of the important men and skilled workers back to Babylon. He also carried away the treasures of the temple and palace.

4 Nebuchadnezzar made Zedekiah king in Jehoiachin's place. But nine years later, Zedekiah also rebelled. So the Babylonian army returned to attack the city of Jerusalem again.

5 After two years of siege, there was nothing left in the city to eat. The people of Jerusalem were starving to death.

6 Finally the Babylonians were able to break holes in the walls of the city. That night Zedekiah and many of his soldiers escaped from the city and slipped through the enemy lines in the darkness.

7 But they were discovered as they raced toward the Jordan valley. The Babylonians captured King Zedekiah near Jericho. All his soldiers deserted him and ran away.

8 The cruel Babylonians made Zedekiah watch as they put his sons to death. Then they put out Zedekiah's eyes and led him off to Babylon in chains, a prisoner.

9 Next the Babylonians entered the city. They burned down the Temple of the Lord and carried off all the objects made of gold, silver, or bronze. They burned the palace and many fine houses.

10 The Babylonian general took the most important priests and officials of the court and commanders of the army to Nebuchadnezzar's camp. There the Babylonians beat them to death.

11 The people of Jerusalem who were still alive were made captives and taken to Babylon. Only the poorest people were left behind to work in the fields and vineyards.

12 Jerusalem and the Temple of the Lord lay in ruins. The people of Judah were taken into exile. The warnings of the prophets had come true. The Lord had punished his people for their sins.

Daniel in Babylon

1 Nebuchadnezzar of Babylon first attacked Jerusalem during Jehoiakim's reign. He took many Israelites back to Babylon as prisoners. One of these prisoners was a young man named Daniel.

2 King Nebuchadnezzar ordered that the finest young Israelites be trained to serve in the royal court. Daniel and his three friends were among those selected for this training.

3 Daniel and his friends didn't eat the king's food. They ate only vegetables and drank only water. But they became stronger and wiser than the others.

4 At the end of the three-year training period, the king was more impressed with Daniel and his friends than with all of the others. So he made these four young men members of the royal court.

5 One night King Nebuchadnezzar had a dream. It worried him greatly, so he called for his fortune tellers and magicians. They said, "Tell us your dream and we will interpret it for you."

6 But the king said, "No, I want you to tell me the dream as well as its meaning. If you can, you will get a reward; but if you can't, I'll have you torn to pieces."

7 "But that's impossible," they said. "Only the gods could do such a thing!" The king was furious and ordered his men to kill all the royal advisers. Even Daniel and his friends were arrested.

8 Daniel asked for time so that he could interpret the dream. He urged his friends to pray that God would make known the mystery. That night God revealed the mystery to Daniel in a vision.

9 Daniel said to the king, "None of the wise men of Babylon could tell you what you dreamed, but there is a God in heaven who reveals mysteries. He has made known what will happen in the future."

10 Daniel said, "You dreamed of a giant statue made of gold, silver, bronze, iron, and clay. A rock hit its feet, and it broke into pieces and blew away. But the rock grew into a mountain."

11 Then he said, "The statue is your kingdom and four kingdoms that will come after yours. The rock that destroys them is the kingdom which God will build. It will last forever."

12 The king bowed low and said, "Your God is the greatest of gods, for he made you able to explain this mystery." He rewarded Daniel by making him the head of all the royal advisers.

The Fiery Furnace

1 After Daniel explained Nebuchadnezzar's dream, the king made him head of all the royal advisers. He also appointed Daniel's three friends to important jobs in the province of Babylon.

2 Nebuchadnezzar later made a statue of gold. It was huge — about ninety feet high! He set it up in the plain of Dura and ordered all his officials to come and celebrate the new statue.

3 At the ceremony a servant announced, "The king commands that when the music begins, everyone must bow down and worship the statue. Anyone who does not will be thrown into a furnace."

4 So when they heard the sound of the musical instruments, all the officials of the empire bowed down and worshiped the golden statue. That is, all but Daniel's three friends.

5 Certain people who hated the Jews told the king, "The three friends of Daniel—Shadrach, Meshach, and Abednego—are disobeying you. They do not worship your statue as you ordered."

6 The king was terribly angry. He called for the three Jews and said, "If you don't bow down, you will be thrown into the furnace right now. There is no god who can save you."

7 They replied, "We won't try to defend ourselves. If the God we serve is able to save us from the furnace, he will. But even if he doesn't, we will not worship your god or bow to the statue."

8 The angry king ordered that the furnace be made seven times hotter than usual. Then they tied up Daniel's three friends and threw them, clothes and all, into the fiery furnace.

9 After a while, the king suddenly leaped to his feet in amazement. He said, "Didn't you throw in *three* men? Why do I see *four* walking around in the fire? The fourth one looks like a god!"

10 Then the king shouted, "Come out!" and out of the furnace came the three Jews. They were not hurt at all by the fire! Not even their clothes were burned!

11 The king said, "Praise the God of Shadrach, Meshach, and Abednego! He sent his angel to rescue these men who serve and trust him. They risked death rather than worship another god!"

12 "From now on, anyone who says anything bad about their God shall be torn apart. No other god can rescue like this!" Then he gave Daniel's friends even more important jobs.

The Writing on the Wall

1 Nebuchadnezzar became ill and was unable to rule over the kingdom of Babylon. So his son Belshazzar became king in his place. One night Belshazzar had a very strange experience.

2 As he drank his wine at a banquet, he had an idea. He ordered his servants to bring the gold and silver cups which his father had taken from the temple of the Lord in Jerusalem.

3 Then the king and his guests drank wine from the cups taken from the Lord's temple, and they praised their gods — idols made of gold and silver, of bronze, iron, wood, and stone.

4 Suddenly Belshazzar saw a human hand writing something on the wall of the banquet hall. He was terrified at the sight. His face turned white and his knees knocked together.

5 Immediately he called for his wise men. "Who can explain this writing? I will give him a purple robe and a golden chain. And I will make him third in command of the kingdom."

6 But none of his wise men or advisers could figure out what the writing meant. This made Belshazzar even more afraid. His guests at the banquet were very confused.

7 Just then the king's mother came in. When she heard what had happened, she said, "Your father made a man named Daniel chief of advisers because of his wisdom. He'll be able to explain it."

8 So Belshazzar called for Daniel and gave him the same promises he had given his wise men. But Daniel said, "I do not want any of these gifts. I will just read the writing and explain it to you."

9 "God made your father a great king. But he became too proud, so his glory and power were taken away. He lived like an animal until he admitted that even kings are under God's rule."

10 "Even though you knew all this, you drank wine from the cups of the temple and worshiped idols made of metal and stone. You did not honor the God who has power over your very life."

11 "This is God's message: MENE means your kingdom is coming to an end. TEKEL means you have fallen short. And PARSIN means your kingdom will be given to the Medes and Persians."

12 Belshazzar then gave Daniel the purple robe and golden chain and made him third in command. That very night Belshazzar was killed, and Darius the Mede took over the kingdom.

Daniel in the Lions' Den

1 On the very night that he had seen the fingers of a human hand writing on the wall of the banquet hall, Belshazzar was killed. The new ruler of Babylon was Darius the Mede.

2 Darius made Daniel one of the three officials who supervised the governors of the land. Daniel was such a good supervisor that Darius was thinking about putting him over the whole kingdom.

3 But the other officials were jealous. They tried to find some fault with Daniel — but they couldn't, because he was an honest man and a good worker. They decided to get him into trouble.

4 These jealous officials went to the king and said, "We think you should order that no one can pray to any god or any man except the king for thirty days. Anyone who disobeys should be killed."

5 When Daniel learned that Darius had signed this order, he went home. He knelt at a window that faced Jerusalem. Then, just as he had always done three times a day, he prayed to the Lord.

6 Daniel's enemies saw him praying at his window. They went straight to the king and said, "Daniel does not respect or obey the king's orders. He still prays three times every day."

7 They insisted that Daniel be punished. The king was quite upset and tried to think of a way to save Daniel. "The king's orders cannot be changed," they reminded him.

8 So Darius ordered Daniel thrown into the lions' den. But he said to Daniel, "I hope your God rescues you." Then they put a stone over the opening and sealed it so no one could help Daniel.

9 That evening the king was so worried about Daniel that he wanted no food or entertainment. He couldn't sleep. At dawn he ran to the den and cried, "Daniel, was your God able to save you?"

10 And Daniel answered! He said, "God sent his angel to shut the mouths of the lions! They have not hurt me! God saved me because he knows that I have done the king no wrong."

11 The king had Daniel pulled out of the lions' den. Then the jealous officials who had accused Daniel were thrown in. The lions immediately leaped on them and killed them.

12 Afterwards, Darius wrote a letter to all his subjects: "Everyone must show respect to the God of Daniel. His God is a god who rescues and saves. He has saved Daniel from the lions."

Esther Becomes Queen

1 When the people of Judah were captives of the Babylonians, the Persian empire destroyed Babylon. Xerxes, the Persian king, was unhappy with his wife. He began to search for a new queen.

2 Many beautiful young women were chosen from all parts of the empire and brought to Susa, the capital city of Persia.

3 Now there was a Jewish girl named Esther who lived in Susa with a relative named Mordecai. She was one of the girls chosen to come before the king. Esther told no one she was Jewish.

4 For a full year the girls were given a special beauty treatment. Then they were presented to the king. Xerxes liked Esther more than all the others and chose her to be his new queen.

5 During that year Mordecai got a job in the palace. One day he happened to overhear a plot: two of the palace guards planned to kill the king. He told Esther, and she told the king.

6 The two guards were arrested and put to death. The king put a report of this matter in his official records. It later turned out to be a good thing for Mordecai that he did so.

7 About five years after Esther became queen of Persia, the Jews of that land faced a great danger. It all began when a man named Haman received a promotion from the king.

8 King Xerxes made Haman greater than anyone else in the land. He even ordered that all his servants must bow down before Haman. But one person refused to do that — Esther's cousin, Mordecai.

9 The other servants asked Mordecai why he did not obey the king. The only explanation he ever gave them was that he was a Jew. Every day they tried to get him to bow down before Haman.

10 Finally, they reported Mordecai to Haman. They wondered if he would let Mordecai get away with this. Haman was furious when he heard that Mordecai refused to bow down before him.

11 Haman wanted to get even with Mordecai. He was so angry that he worked out a plan to kill not only Mordecai but all the Jews living in Persia.

12 He persuaded King Xerxes that all the Jews were unlawful and should be destroyed. A decree was issued: "On the thirteenth day of the twelfth month, all the Jews will be put to death."

Esther Goes Before the King

1 When Mordecai heard of Haman's plan to kill all the Jews, he wept and tore his clothing. Esther sent a servant to find out what was wrong with Mordecai.

2 Mordecai told the servant everything and gave him a copy of Haman's decree that the Jews be killed. He said, "Show this to Esther. Tell her to beg the king to have mercy on her people."

3 Esther answered Mordecai: "Anyone who goes to King Xerxes without being called by him will be killed! Only if the king holds out his scepter will that person be spared! Everyone knows this!"

4 Mordecai warned her, "Don't think you are safer than other Jews. If you keep quiet, you too will be killed. But it may be that you became queen for just such a time as this."

5 So Esther sent this message to Mordecai: "Have all the Jews of Susa fast and pray for three days and nights. Then I will go to the king. If I must die, then I will die."

6 On the third day of the fast, Esther went to the courtyard of the palace. King Xerxes saw her standing outside the door — and held out his scepter toward her!

7 So Esther went safely up to the king. "Tell me what you want," he said. "I'll give you anything you ask for — even half of my kingdom."

8 "If it please the king," she said, "I would like for you and Haman to be my guests at a banquet today." So the king called for Haman, and together they attended Esther's banquet.

9 Xerxes again said, "Tell me what you want, and you shall have it." But Esther said, "I'd like for you and Haman to be my guests again tomorrow at another banquet. At that time I'll tell you."

10 Haman left the banquet in a very good mood. But then he saw Mordecai near the palace. Mordecai didn't get up or show him any respect. Haman was furious, but he didn't say a word.

11 Haman called his friends together and boasted, "Tomorrow the queen is giving a banquet just for the king and me." But then he said, "As long as Mordecai lives, I can never be really happy."

12 His friends said, "Why not build a gallows and ask the king to hang Mordecai on it? Then you can enjoy the banquet." Haman liked this idea and made plans to hang Mordecai the very next day.

Haman's Plans Go Wrong

1 On the very night that Haman was making plans to hang Mordecai, King Xerxes was unable to go to sleep. So he had his servants bring the official records of the empire and read them to him.

2 When they read how Mordecai had saved the king's life by warning of a murder plot, the king stopped them. He asked, "What was done to thank Mordecai?" They replied, "Nothing at all."

3 Just then Haman came in to ask the king to hang Mordecai on the gallows he had built. When the servants told the king that Haman was waiting to see him, the king said, "Send him in."

4 The king said to Haman, "There is someone I wish to honor. What should I do for this man?" Haman thought to himself, "The king must be going to honor *me*!"

5 So Haman said, "Dress the man in your royal robes and have your highest nobleman lead him through the city square on your horse saying, 'Thus does the king honor this man.'"

6 Then the king said, "That's good, Haman. Now hurry and get my robe and horse and give all these to Mordecai the Jew. Do everything for him that you have suggested."

7 So Haman had to give Mordecai the honors he expected for himself! Afterward, Haman went home hiding his face in anger and shame. Soon the king's servants arrived to take him to the banquet.

8 As Haman and King Xerxes ate with Esther, the king again asked her, "What is it you want? Tell me and you shall have it — even up to half of my kingdom."

9 Esther answered, "My people and I are about to be destroyed! Please save us!" Xerxes was shocked and said, "Who would dare to do such a thing?" "Our enemy is Haman," Esther replied.

10 Haman was terrified. The king was so angry that he left the room and went out to the palace gardens. Fearing the king would punish him, Haman stayed behind to beg Queen Esther to save him.

11 Just as Haman threw himself on Esther's couch to beg for mercy, the king came back in. Seeing Haman, he was even more angry. "Will he attack the queen in my own palace?" he shouted.

12 Xerxes had the evil Haman hanged on the gallows built for Mordecai. Then he issued a new decree allowing the Jews to defend themselves. A time of sadness became a time of joy for God's people.

Nehemiah Rebuilds the Walls

1 Nehemiah was one of the Jewish exiles who lived in Persia when Artaxerxes was king. He was an important official in the king's house in Susa.

2 One day Nehemiah's brother came to Susa. He described how difficult life was for the Jews now living in Jerusalem. The walls were still in ruins and the gates had not been replaced.

3 This news upset Nehemiah. But he had an idea and prayed for God's help. About four months later the king asked Nehemiah why he looked so sad. He said, "Because Jerusalem still lies in ruins."

4 Then Nehemiah said, "Please let me go back to my country so I can help rebuild Jerusalem." The king granted his request and gave him some letters that would help him when he got there.

5 Three days after he arrived in Jerusalem, Nehemiah got up in the middle of the night. He rode around the south part of the city, examining the condition of the walls.

6 Then Nehemiah talked with the Jewish leaders. "Look at how many problems we are having because our city is in ruins. Let's rebuild the walls!" The leaders agreed and said, "Let's get to work."

7 But the enemies of the Jews were angry when they heard of this. Sanballat and Tobiah made fun and said, "Are you going to rebel against the king?" Nehemiah just said, "God will help us."

8 Each part of the wall and each gate was assigned to a certain group of workers. Priests, metal workers, merchants—all kinds of people helped. Even people from other towns helped.

9 When the walls were almost half finished, Sanballat made plans to attack the Jews. However, Nehemiah heard about it and posted guards both day and night. Sanballat had to give up his plans.

10 But from then on, half of the Jews stood guard while the others worked. Even the ones who were working carried weapons. At night everyone stayed in the city to guard it from attack.

11 Sanballat next tried to blackmail Nehemiah with false rumors that would get him in trouble with the king of Persia. But Nehemiah was not frightened. He just prayed and kept the work going.

12 After fifty-two days the work was finished. The walls and gates had been completely rebuilt. Everyone, even the enemies of the Jews, knew that this could not have been done without God's help.

An Angel Visits Zechariah

1 Hundreds of years had passed since the Jews had returned from exile to their homeland. But foreign kings continued to rule over them. The land of Israel was now a part of the great Roman Empire.

2 The Jews longed for freedom. They dreamed of the day when the new kingdom promised by the prophets would come. They waited for the Messiah (Christ) to save them and rule over them.

3 In those days there was a priest named Zechariah. He and his wife Elizabeth were fine people who obeyed the laws of God. But they had never had any children, and now they were very old.

4 Zechariah's turn came to serve as a priest in Jerusalem. While he was burning incense in the Temple, he suddenly saw an angel standing by the altar. Zechariah was surprised and frightened.

5 The angel said, "Don't be afraid. God has heard your prayer. You and Elizabeth will have a baby boy. You shall name him John. He will be a great man in God's sight."

6 "He will bring many Israelites back to the Lord. He will go ahead of the Lord like the prophet Elijah. He will get the people ready for the Lord."

7 Zechariah said, "How can I be sure of this?" The angel said, "It was God who sent me with this good news. Since you have not believed it, you will be unable to speak until it comes true."

8 The people standing outside the Temple wondered why Zechariah stayed inside so long. When he came out he could not speak, so they knew that he must have seen a vision.

9 At the end of his duties, Zechariah went home. In time Elizabeth had a baby—a boy, just as the angel had said. Elizabeth was overjoyed that the Lord had given her a child. Her friends rejoiced, too.

10 When the baby was a week old, he was circumcised. At that time they gave him a name. Their friends thought they would name him after his father. But Elizabeth said, "His name will be John."

11 They were surprised and asked Zechariah what he wanted to name the child. Zechariah wrote on a tablet, "His name is John." At that very moment Zechariah became able to talk again.

12 The child named John grew up and became strong in body and spirit. He lived apart from other people in the desert until the day he began to preach to the people of Israel.

An Angel Visits Mary

1 About six months after Zechariah and Elizabeth learned that they would have a baby, God sent an angel to a girl named Mary at Nazareth. She was engaged to marry a man named Joseph.

2 The angel said: "Peace be with you. The Lord has greatly blessed you." Mary was confused and wondered what the angel meant. "God is very pleased with you," the angel continued.

3 "You are going to have a baby boy, and you shall name him Jesus. He will be called the Son of the Most High. God will make him a king like his ancestor David. His kingdom will never end."

4 "But I am not yet married," Mary said. "How can this be?" The angel answered, "The Holy Spirit will come and God's power will rest upon you. Therefore, the child will be called the Son of God."

5 So Mary said, "I am the Lord's servant. May it be as you have said." Then the angel went away.

6 Soon after that, Mary went to visit Elizabeth, who was her relative. When Elizabeth heard Mary's greeting, she felt her baby move within her.

7 Then Elizabeth was filled with the Holy Spirit and said, "You are the most blessed of all women. And blessed is the child you will bear."

8 Mary said, "My heart praises the Lord. All people will call me blessed because of the great things God has done for me." Mary stayed with Elizabeth three months and then returned home.

9 When Joseph learned that Mary was going to have a baby, he was very unhappy. Joseph decided to quietly break his engagement with Mary. He did not want to disgrace Mary before other people.

10 But before he had done anything about this, an angel appeared to him in a dream. The angel said, "Joseph, do not be afraid to take Mary as your wife. The child in her is from the Holy Spirit."

11 "She will give birth to a boy," the angel continued. "You shall name him Jesus, because he will save his people from their sins." After this dream, Joseph went ahead and took Mary to be his wife.

12 All this happened so that what the Lord said through the prophet Isaiah would come true: "A virgin will have a son and they will call him Immanuel (which means 'God with us')."

The Messiah Is Born

1 Months had passed since the angel told Mary that she would have a baby. Word now came that Augustus, emperor of Rome, had ordered everyone to go to his hometown and sign a roll book.

2 So Joseph took Mary and went from Nazareth to Bethlehem of Judea, where he had been born. It was there that King David, Joseph's ancestor, had been born hundreds of years before.

3 While they were in Bethlehem, the time came for Mary's baby to be born. Because all the inns were full, they had to stay in a stable. Mary used a manger as a bed for the baby.

4 That same night an angel of the Lord appeared to some shepherds who were in the fields with their sheep. The glory of the Lord shone around them and they were afraid.

5 But the angel said, "I have brought you very good news. This very day your Savior was born in the city of David. He is Christ, the Lord. You will find him lying in a manger."

6 The shepherds hurried to Bethlehem. There they found Joseph and Mary—and the baby lying in a manger.

7 The shepherds told them all that the angel had said about the child. The words filled them with amazement. Mary remembered these things and thought about them deeply.

8 When the child was one week old, they took him to be circumcised. At that time, they named him Jesus, just as the angel had instructed them to do.

9 After forty days, Joseph and Mary went to Jerusalem. They sacrificed a pair of doves or pigeons, as the Law required. While they were in the Temple, an old man named Simeon came up.

10 Simeon was a good man who was hoping for the salvation of Israel. The Holy Spirit had promised him that he would not die before he saw the Messiah whom God had promised.

11 Simeon took Jesus in his arms and gave thanks to God. He said, "Lord, you have kept your promise; now I can die in peace. With my own eyes I have seen your salvation."

12 He said to Mary, "This child will cause the rise and fall of many in Israel. Many will speak against him, and your own heart will be broken with sorrow." Mary and Joseph were amazed at his words.

The Wise Men

1 After Jesus was born, some wise men from a country in the east arrived in Jerusalem. These were men who studied and looked for signs in the stars.

2 When they got to Jerusalem, they asked, "Where is the baby who was born to be the king of the Jews? We saw his star in the east, and we have come to worship him."

3 Herod, the king of Judea, was very upset when he heard what the wise men were saying. He called for the chief priests and the teachers of the Law and asked, "Where will the Messiah be born?"

4 "He will be born in Bethlehem of Judea," they answered. "The prophet Micah wrote, 'Out of you (Bethlehem) will come a ruler who will be the shepherd of my people Israel.'"

5 Herod met in secret with the wise men to find out exactly when they first saw the star. Then he said, "When you find the child, let me know. I, too, want to go and worship him."

6 As the wise men set out, the star they had seen in the east appeared again. They were filled with joy. The star went before them and led them to the place where Jesus was.

7 When the wise men entered, they saw Mary with the child. They bowed down and worshiped him. Then they opened the gifts that they had brought for Jesus—gold and incense and perfume.

8 But when they left there, they did not return to King Herod. They had been warned in a dream not to go back. Instead, they returned to their own country by a different way.

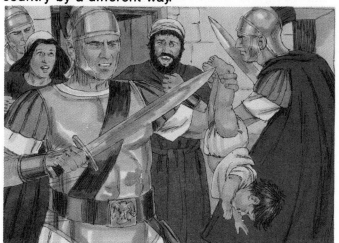

9 An angel also warned Joseph through a dream. He said, "Joseph, get up and take the child and his mother to Egypt. Stay there until I tell you, for Herod is going to try to kill the child."

10 When Herod realized that the wise men had tricked him, he was furious. He ordered his men to kill all the little boys in Bethlehem who were not yet two years old. It was a time of great sorrow.

11 After some time, Herod died. Then the angel again appeared to Joseph in a dream and said, "You can take the boy and his mother back to the land of Israel, for they will now be safe."

12 So they returned to the land of Israel. But when Joseph heard that Herod's son was now the ruler of Judea, he was afraid to go there. So they settled in the town of Nazareth in Galilee.

The Boy Jesus

1 King Herod wanted to kill the child born to be "king of the Jews," so Joseph took Mary and Jesus to Egypt for a while. After Herod died, they returned to the land of Israel and settled in Galilee.

2 Thus Jesus grew up in the town of Nazareth with his mother Mary and her husband Joseph. The boy become strong and wise. And he was blessed by God.

3 Now, each year Joseph and Mary went to Jerusalem in order to celebrate the Passover. When Jesus was twelve years old, they took him with them on the long trip to Jerusalem.

4 When the feast of Passover was ended, Mary and Joseph left for home. They thought Jesus was with the others in their group. They did not know that he had stayed behind in Jerusalem.

5 They traveled for about a day before they missed Jesus. They checked with all their friends and relatives, but no one had seen the boy. So they turned back to Jerusalem.

6 Joseph and Mary searched all over the city for Jesus. Then, after three days, they found him. He was in the Temple!

7 Jesus was sitting among the teachers of the Law, listening to them and asking them questions. Everyone there was amazed at how much he understood and how well he answered.

8 Mary and Joseph were quite surprised to find their son there.

9 "My son, why have you treated us this way?" Mary said to him. "Your father and I have been very worried about you! We've looked everywhere for you!"

10 Jesus replied, "Why did you have to look for me? Didn't you know I would be in my Father's house?" Joseph and Mary did not really understand what Jesus meant by these words.

11 Then Jesus went back to Nazareth with his mother and Joseph. He was always obedient to his parents. His mother remembered all these things.

12 Jesus grew in mind and body. And he grew in favor with God and man.

John Prepares the Way

1 John, the child born to Zechariah and Elizabeth a few months before Jesus was born, grew and became strong in both body and spirit.

2 He lived in the desert and wore clothes made from camel's hair. He had a leather belt around his waist. For food he ate locusts and wild honey.

3 There in the desert, the Word of God came to John. This happened in the fifteenth year of the Emperor Tiberius, when Pilate was governor of Judea and Herod was ruler of Galilee.

4 Then John began to preach to the Jewish people. He went throughout the whole area around the Jordan River, saying, "Turn away from your sins and be baptized, and God will forgive you."

5 Crowds came from Jerusalem and all of Judea to the Jordan River where John was baptizing. When he saw many of the Pharisees and Sadducees coming for baptism, he spoke sharply to them.

6 "You bunch of snakes! Don't think you can escape punishment just because you are descendants of Abraham! God could take these rocks and make them into descendants of Abraham!"

7 The people said, "Then what are we to do?" And John replied, "Whoever has two garments must give one to the man who has none, and whoever has food must share it."

8 Some tax collectors came to John to be baptized and they asked him, "Teacher, what are we to do?" John replied, "Don't collect more tax money than you are supposed to."

9 Some soldiers asked John what they should do. He answered, "Don't take money from anyone by force or make false accusations. Be happy with the pay you get."

10 People began to wonder whether John might be the Messiah. John denied it. "Someone is coming who is greater than I am," he said. "I am not good enough even to untie his sandals."

11 "I baptize you with water, but he will baptize you with the Holy Spirit and fire. He will thresh out the grain and gather the wheat into his barn—but the chaff he will burn."

12 This John was indeed the man Isaiah meant when he said, "Someone is shouting in the desert: 'Get the road ready for the Lord.'"

Jesus' Baptism and Temptation

1 When John the Baptist began to preach near the Jordan River, great crowds came to hear him. Those who believed what John preached were baptized by him in the river.

2 Jesus was one of those who came to John to be baptized. But John was surprised when he saw Jesus. He tried to stop Jesus, saying, "I need to be baptized by *you*! Why do you come to me?"

3 Jesus answered John, "Let it be so, for this is what God wants us to do." So John baptized Jesus.

4 As Jesus came up out of the water, he saw the Spirit of God coming down like a dove and alighting upon him. A voice from heaven said, "This is my own dear Son. I am pleased with him."

5 Right away the Spirit of God led Jesus into the desert. For forty days and nights he ate nothing at all. Then the devil came to see if he could cause Jesus to sin.

6 Because Jesus had not eaten for so long, he was very hungry. So the devil said to him, "If you really are the Son of God, turn these stones into bread."

7 Jesus replied, "The Scriptures say, 'Man does not live on bread alone, but on every word that God speaks.' "

8 Then the devil took Jesus to the top of the Temple. "If you are the Son of God, throw yourself down. The Scriptures say, 'His angels will not let you strike your foot against a stone.' "

9 Jesus answered, "The Scriptures *also* say, 'Do not put the Lord your God to the test.' "

10 Then the devil took him to a very high mountain. He showed Jesus all the kingdoms of the world. "All this will be yours," the devil said, "if you will just bow down and worship me."

11 But Jesus replied, "Get away from me, Satan. The Scriptures say, 'Worship the Lord your God and serve no one but him.' "

12 Then the devil left him and angels came and cared for him.

Jesus' First Disciples

1 John had been surprised to see Jesus among the crowds of people who came to be baptized. At first he had not wanted to baptize Jesus, but Jesus told him that was what God wanted.

2 Later, John was standing with two of his disciples (followers) when he saw Jesus walking by. He said to them, "Look, the Lamb of God."

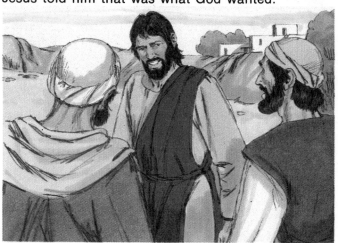

3 Hearing these words the two men started to follow Jesus. When Jesus turned and saw them, he asked, "What do you want?" "Teacher, where are you staying?" they replied.

4 "Come and see," Jesus said. So they went with him to see where he was living. This was about four o'clock in the afternoon. They spent the rest of the day with Jesus.

5 One of these men was Andrew. He had a brother named Simon Peter. The first thing Andrew did after he left Jesus was to find Simon and say, "We have found the Messiah (the Christ)!"

6 Then he took Simon to where Jesus was. Jesus looked at Simon and said, "You are Simon, the son of John. You will be called Peter."

7 The next day Jesus decided to leave for Galilee. Then he found a young man named Philip and said to him, "Follow me." Like Andrew and Peter, Philip was from the town of Bethsaida.

8 Philip went to look for Nathanael. He told him, "We have found the man about whom Moses and the prophets wrote! He is Jesus of Nazareth."

9 "Nazareth!" exclaimed Nathanael. "Can anything good come from there?" "Come and see," Philip replied.

10 When Jesus saw Nathanael coming with Philip, he said, "Here is a true Israelite. There is nothing false in him."

11 "How do you know me?" Nathanael asked. Jesus answered, "I saw you while you were still under the fig tree, before Philip called you."

12 Amazed, Nathanael said, "Teacher, you are the Son of God, the King of Israel!" Jesus replied, "You believe because I said I saw you under the fig tree? You shall see greater things than that!"

The Wedding at Cana

1 Four men had now become followers (or disciples) of Jesus. Their names were Andrew, Simon Peter (he was Andrew's brother), Philip, and Nathanael.

2 A few days after they began to go about with Jesus, there was a wedding in the village of Cana. Jesus and his followers were invited to attend. Jesus' mother was there, too.

3 During the wedding feast an embarrassing thing happened—the host ran out of wine. Jesus' mother came to Jesus and said, "They have no more wine."

4 "What does this have to do with me?" Jesus replied. "My time has not yet come." But his mother said to the servants, "Do whatever he tells you."

5 Nearby were six stone water jars. These jars were used by the Jews for their religious ceremonies. Each held about twenty or thirty gallons.

6 Jesus said to the servants, "Fill these jars with water." So they filled each jar to the very top.

7 Then Jesus said, "Now dip out some and take it to the man in charge of the wedding feast."

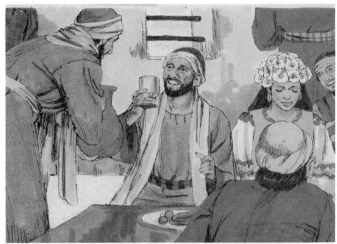

8 When the man in charge tasted it, the water had already become wine! He didn't know where this wine had come from. The servants knew, of course.

9 Then the man in charge called aside the man who had just been married. He said, "People always serve the best wine first."

10 "Then when everyone has gotten drunk, they serve the cheaper wine. But you have saved the best until last!"

11 This was the first of the miracles that Jesus did as signs of who he was. His glory was revealed there at Cana. And his followers believed in him.

12 After the wedding Jesus left for Capernaum with his mother and his brothers and his disciples. They stayed there for several days.

A Woman of Samaria

1 After the wedding at Cana, Jesus spent a few days at Capernaum and then went to Jerusalem for the Passover celebration. At the end of the feast, Jesus and his disciples started back to Galilee.

2 They came to a town in Samaria called Sychar. Nearby was a well known as "Jacob's well." At noon Jesus was tired, so he sat down by the well while the disciples went into town to buy food.

3 While they were gone, a Samaritan woman came to draw water. Jesus said, "Let me have a drink of water." She was surprised. "Why do you, a Jew, ask me, a Samaritan, for a drink?" she asked.

4 Jesus said, "If you knew who I am, you would have asked me for 'living water.'" "This is a deep well and you have nothing to draw water with," she said. "Where will you get this 'living water'?"

5 Jesus said, "Everyone who drinks this water will get thirsty again. But no one who drinks the water I give him will ever be thirsty again."

6 She said, "Give me that water so I won't get thirsty and have to keep coming back to this well." Jesus said, "Go get your husband and bring him here."

7 "I have no husband," she replied. Jesus said, "You have told the truth. The fact is that you have had five husbands, and the man you are now living with is *not* your husband."

8 "I can see that you are a prophet," she said, changing the subject. "Our ancestors have always worshiped on this mountain, but you Jews say that we must worship in Jerusalem."

9 Jesus said, "The time is coming when people will not have to worship in Jerusalem or on this mountain. True worshipers will worship God in spirit and in truth, for that is what God wants."

10 She said, "I know that the Messiah is coming. And when he comes, he will explain everything to us." "I am he," Jesus said.

11 Then the woman went back to town, forgetting her water jar. She said to everyone, "Come see a man who told me everything I ever did. Can this be the Messiah?" They came out to see Jesus.

12 Many Samaritans believed in Jesus because of the woman. But after he was with them for two days, some of them said to her, "Now we've heard for ourselves. We know this man really is the Savior!"

The Centurion's Faith

1 In the time of Jesus, Rome ruled over the land of Palestine. Roman soldiers were stationed at different places throughout the country to keep the peace.

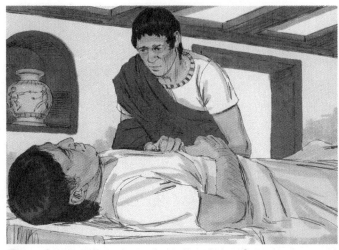

2 A certain centurion lived in Capernaum. (A centurion was an officer in charge of one hundred soldiers.) This centurion had a servant who was very dear to him. The servant was very sick.

3 When the centurion heard of Jesus, he asked some of the Jewish leaders of the city to go and talk to Jesus for him.

4 These leaders urged Jesus to heal the centurion's servant. They said, "This man deserves your help. Although he is a Gentile, he loves the Jewish people. He even built a synagogue for us."

5 So Jesus went with the Jewish leaders to the centurion's house. When they were not far off, the centurion saw them coming and sent out some friends. "Give Jesus this message," he told them.

6 The message said: "Lord, I am not worthy to have you come into my house. This is why I sent other people instead of coming myself. If you just say the word, I know my servant will be healed."

7 "I also am a man with authority," the message continued. "If I say to one of my soldiers, 'Go!' he goes. If I say to another, 'Come!' he comes. If I say to my servant, 'Do this!' he does it."

8 Jesus was very surprised at the centurion's words. He turned to those who were following him and said, "I have not found such faith as this even among the people of Israel!"

9 Jesus went on, saying, "Many people from all the world will come to sit down with Abraham, Isaac, and Jacob for the banquet in the kingdom of God."

10 "But the sons of the kingdom who ought to be there will be thrown out of the banquet hall into the darkness outside. There they will cry out and grind their teeth."

11 Jesus said to the friends whom the centurion had sent to him, "Tell the centurion that it shall be done for him as he has believed."

12 Then Jesus sent the centurion's friends back to the house. When they got there, they found that the servant was already well!

Jesus Forgives Sins

1 One day, after preaching and teaching at different places, Jesus returned to Capernaum. The news spread through town that Jesus had come home.

2 Many people came to his house to see him. The crowd was so great that the house was filled and no one else could even get inside the door. Jesus was preaching to the people who had come.

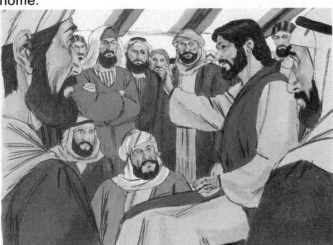

3 Among those who came to listen were some scribes (teachers of the Law) and Pharisees. They came from all parts of the country — from the villages of Galilee and Judea, and even Jerusalem.

4 Four men arrived carrying a man on his bed. The man was paralyzed; he could not move his legs at all. They had brought him to be healed, but because of the crowds they couldn't get inside.

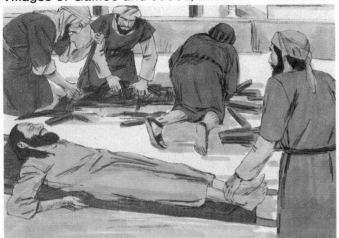

5 Then one of them said, "Let's lower him down through the roof!" So they carried the man up to the roof and dug a big hole in it.

6 Then they lowered the paralyzed man down into the room right in front of Jesus!

7 When Jesus saw their faith, he said to the man who was paralyzed, "My son, your sins are forgiven."

8 Some of the scribes and Pharisees began to say to themselves, "How can he say such a thing? He's insulting God! Nobody but God can forgive sins!"

9 Jesus knew what they were thinking. He said to them, "Why do you have such thoughts? Which is easier to say — 'Your sins are forgiven' or 'Rise, take up your bed, and walk'?"

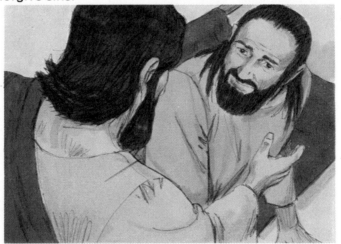

10 "Now so you'll know that the Son of man has authority on earth to forgive sins" — he turned toward the paralyzed man and said, "Get up, and take your bed, and go home."

11 Immediately the man who had been unable to walk got up! He picked up his bed and went walking out through the crowded room.

12 When the people saw this they were amazed. They praised God and said, "We've never seen anything like this before!"

Jesus Chooses the Twelve

1 Already Jesus had called six men to follow him. Their names were Simon (Peter), Andrew, James, John, Philip, and Nathanael. These were his first disciples.

2 One day, after Jesus finished teaching beside the Sea of Galilee, he passed by a collection booth where the Jews paid their taxes to the Romans. He noticed one of the tax collectors, who was a Jew.

3 Jesus spoke to this man, saying, "Follow me." The man got up and followed Jesus, leaving everything there behind him. This tax collector's name was Levi. He is also known as Matthew.

4 Levi held a feast for Jesus at his house. While they were eating, some of Levi's friends came in. They sat down and began to eat and visit with Jesus and his disciples.

5 Now Levi's friends were also tax collectors and people who did not carefully keep the Jewish laws. The Pharisees, who thought such people were sinners, heard that Jesus was eating with them.

6 This angered the Pharisees greatly. They said to Jesus' disciples, "Why does your teacher eat with tax collectors and sinners?"

7 Jesus heard their question. He said, "People who are well don't need a doctor, but those who are sick do. I didn't come to call those who are already doing right, but those who are sinning."

8 One day after Jesus had preached and healed for quite a while, he went up into the hills. He spent the night there praying. The next day he called certain of his followers to him.

9 Jesus appointed these twelve disciples to be his apostles (or special messengers): Peter and his brother, Andrew; James and his brother, John (Jesus called these two the Sons of Thunder);

10 Philip and Bartholomew (perhaps another name for Nathanael); Matthew (the tax collector also known as Levi); Thomas (also called the Twin); another James (the son of Alphaeus);

11 Thaddaeus (also known as Judas, the son of James); and another Simon (also called the Zealot). There was another Judas, too — Judas Iscariot. This is the man who later betrayed Jesus.

12 Jesus chose these twelve men to be with him and to go out and preach. He gave them authority to cast out evil spirits and the power to heal the sick. He trained them to carry on his work.

The Sermon on the Mount

1 As Jesus' fame spread, people came from all over the country to see him. One day he went up on a mountain and preached to his disciples. The crowds watched and listened as he taught.

2 "Blessed are the poor in spirit, for theirs is the kingdom of heaven. Blessed are the pure in heart, for they will see God. Blessed are the peacemakers, for they shall be called God's children."

3 "Do not think that I have come to abolish the Law or the Prophets; I have come to fulfill them. Whoever practices and teaches these commands will be called great in the kingdom."

4 "You have heard that it was said long ago, 'Do not murder; anyone who murders will be subject to judgment.' But I tell you that anyone who is angry with his brother will be judged."

5 "You have heard that it was said, 'An eye for an eye and a tooth for a tooth.' But I tell you, Don't resist an evil person. If he strikes you on the right cheek, turn the other to him also."

6 "You have heard it said, 'Love your neighbor and hate your enemy.' But I tell you, Love your enemies and pray for those who persecute you, so you may be children of your Father in heaven."

7 "When you give to the needy, don't announce it with trumpets, as the hypocrites do in the synagogues and streets, to be honored by men. I tell you they have gotten all the reward they'll get."

8 "Don't store up for yourselves treasures on earth, where moth and rust destroy, and where thieves break in and steal. But store up for yourselves treasures in heaven."

9 "Ask and it will be given to you; seek and you will find; knock and the door will be opened. For everyone who asks, receives; he who seeks finds; and to him who knocks, the door will be opened."

10 "In everything, do to others what you would have them do to you. For this is the sum of the Law and the Prophets."

11 "Not everyone who says to me, 'Lord, Lord,' will enter the kingdom of heaven, but only he who does the will of my Father who is in heaven."

12 The crowds were amazed by Jesus' teaching. He taught them not as the scribes, but as one who had authority.

The Parable of the Sower

1 One day when Jesus was sitting beside the sea, a crowd began to gather around him. So Jesus got into a boat, and while the crowd stood on the shore, he taught them in parables.

2 "A sower went out to sow some seed in his field," he said. "But some of the seeds fell along the path. The birds immediately flew down and ate them."

3 "Other seeds fell on rocky ground where there was not much soil. The seeds quickly sprouted. But when the sun came up, they were scorched. Their roots didn't go deep, and they just dried up."

4 "Other seeds fell on thorny ground. The thorns choked out the seeds when they started growing, so they didn't produce any grain, either."

5 "Other seeds fell on good soil, and brought forth great amounts of grain — some thirty-fold, some sixty-fold, and some a hundred-fold. He who has ears, let him hear."

6 Then the disciples came to him and asked, "Why do you speak to the crowds in parables?"

7 Jesus replied, "To you it has been given to know the secrets of the kingdom of heaven. But to them it has not been given. They hear but do not understand, lest they repent and be forgiven."

8 "But you my disciples are truly fortunate, because you are seeing what the prophets and righteous men of old longed to see and hear." Then Jesus explained the parable to the disciples.

9 "The seed is the word of God," he said. "The ones along the path are those who hear the word but do not understand it. Satan quickly comes and takes away the word from their hearts."

10 "Those sown on rocky ground are people who hear the word and immediately receive it with joy. But they have no root in themselves and so when troubles and suffering come along, they fall away."

11 "Those sown among thorns are people who hear the word but the cares of the world and the desire for money choke the word so that it cannot bear fruit."

12 "As for what was sown on good soil, these are people who hear the word and understand it. They bear fruit, some yielding thirty-fold, some sixty-fold, and some a hundred-fold."

The Power of Jesus

1 One day when evening came, Jesus got into a boat with his disciples.

2 He said to them, "Let's go across to the other side of the sea." So they left the crowds and began sailing for the opposite shore. Other boats were also with them.

3 Now while they were crossing the Sea of Galilee, a great storm suddenly arose. The waves beat against the boat and water poured into it.

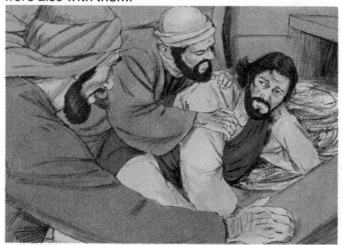

4 The disciples were frightened, but Jesus was asleep in the back of the boat. The disciples woke him up and said, "Teacher, we're about to sink! Don't you care if we die? Save us!"

5 Jesus got up and scolded the wind and sea. "Be quiet! Be still!" he commanded.

6 When Jesus gave this command, the storm stopped and there was a great calm. Then Jesus said to his disciples, "Why are you afraid? Don't you have any faith?"

7 The disciples were filled with awe. They said to one another, "Who is this man that even the wind and the sea obey him?"

8 On another occasion, a man possessed by a demon was brought to Jesus. The man was not able to see or to talk. But Jesus healed this man.

9 The people were amazed and said, "Can Jesus be the Son of David?" But the Pharisees said, "This man is casting out demons because he has the power of Beelzebub, the prince of demons."

10 Jesus knew what the Pharisees were thinking about him. So he said, "If Satan's kingdom is divided against itself, how will his kingdom stand?"

11 "And if I cast out demons by the power of Beelzebub, by whose power do your sons cast them out?"

12 "But if it is by the power of God, then that shows that the kingdom of God has come upon you. It is a sign that someone stronger than Satan has come and is taking away what belonged to Satan."

Jesus Raises Jairus's Daughter

1 Jesus was at the seaside in Capernaum surrounded by a crowd of people, when one of the synagogue rulers came to him. The ruler's name was Jairus.

2 Falling at Jesus' feet, Jairus said, "My little daughter is dying. Please come and put your hands on her so that she will be healed and live." So Jesus went with him.

3 The crowd followed and pressed around Jesus. Among them there was a woman who had suffered from bleeding for twelve years. She had spent all her money on doctors but only got worse.

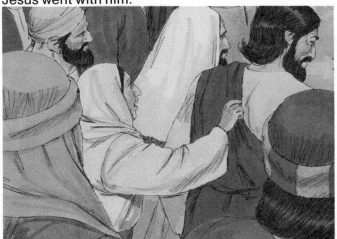

4 She came up behind Jesus in the crowd. "If I just touch his clothes," she thought, "I'll be healed." When she touched his cloak, she could feel in her body that she had indeed been healed.

5 Jesus also knew something had happened. He turned around and said, "Who touched my clothes?" The disciples said, "How can you ask that? Look at all these people!"

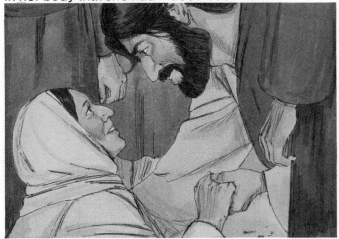

6 But Jesus kept looking around, so the woman came and fell at his feet. Trembling with fear, she told him her story. Then he said, "Daughter, your faith has saved you. Go in peace."

7 While Jesus was still talking to this woman, some men came from the house of Jairus. They said to him, "Your daughter is dead. Why bother the teacher any more?"

8 Jesus paid no attention to what they had said. He turned to Jairus and said, "Don't be afraid. Just believe." Then Jesus allowed only Peter, James, and John to go with him to Jairus' house.

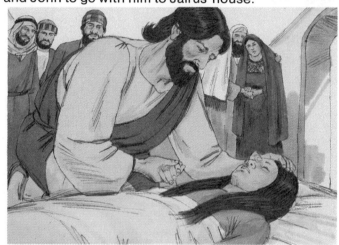

9 When they got there, people were crying and weeping loudly. Jesus said, "Why all this noise and crying? The child is not dead but asleep." They just laughed at him.

10 He put everyone out of the house except Peter, James, John, and the girl's parents. Then he went into the room where she lay.

11 Taking the child by the hand, Jesus said, "Little girl, I say to you, Get up!" Immediately she stood up and walked around. She was about twelve years old.

12 Her parents were amazed. Jesus gave them strict orders not to tell anyone what had happened. Then he told them, "Give her something to eat."

Feeding the Five Thousand

1 After learning from Jesus, Jesus' followers went out to preach to others for a time. Then they returned to their Teacher. "Let's go away and rest for a while," Jesus said.

2 So they got into a boat and sailed for the other side of the Sea of Galilee. But the crowds saw Jesus and his disciples leave.

3 Some of the people from all the nearby towns ran along the shore until they got to the place where Jesus was headed. When the boat landed, Jesus found a great crowd of people waiting for him.

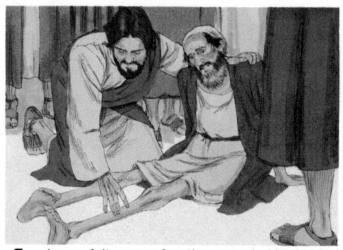

4 Jesus felt sorry for the crowd. He healed people who were sick and taught them many things.

5 When evening came, the disciples said to Jesus, "It's getting late, and there is nothing here for the people to eat. You'd better send them away so they can buy some food in the villages."

6 But Jesus replied, "*You* give them something to eat." His orders shocked the disciples.

7 They said, "It would take hundreds of dollars to get enough bread for all these people! Do you want us to spend that much to buy them food?"

8 "How much bread do you have?" Jesus asked. "Go and check." They came back and said, "We have only five loaves of bread and just two fish."

9 Then Jesus commanded everyone to sit down on the grass. He had them sit in groups of fifty or a hundred people. In all, there were five thousand men, not counting the women and children.

10 Jesus took the bread and fish from the disciples. Then he looked up into heaven and gave thanks to God.

11 After his prayer, Jesus broke the bread and the fish into pieces. He gave this to the disciples, who passed it out to the people sitting in the groups. Everyone ate until he was full.

12 After all had finished, the disciples gathered up what was left. They collected twelve full baskets of bread and fish!

Jesus Walks on the Sea

1 After Jesus fed the great crowd with the five loaves and two fish, he had his disciples get into the boat and go on back to the other side of the Sea of Galilee.

2 Jesus himself stayed behind to dismiss the crowds. After sending them away, he went up into the hills by himself to pray.

3 When evening came, he was alone on the hill. The boat in which the disciples were sailing was now far out on the Sea of Galilee.

4 A strong wind had arisen and the waves were beating against the boat. Jesus could see that they were having trouble rowing because the wind was blowing in the wrong direction.

5 About the fourth watch of the night (from 3:00 to 6:00 in the morning, while it was still dark), Jesus came to the disciples, walking upon the sea!

6 When the disciples saw him coming across the water, they were terrified. "It's a ghost!" they cried.

7 Immediately Jesus spoke to them. He said, "Have courage! It is I. Don't be afraid."

8 Then Peter said, "Lord, if it really is you, order me to come to you on the water." Jesus answered, "Come."

9 So Peter got out of the boat and started walking across the water to Jesus!

10 But when Peter saw the wind, he was afraid and he began to sink. He cried out, "Lord, save me!"

11 Jesus quickly reached out his hand and caught Peter. "O man of little faith, why did you doubt?" he said.

12 When Jesus and Peter got into the boat, the wind stopped blowing. The astonished disciples said, "You truly are the Son of God!" And they worshiped Jesus.

The Transfiguration of Jesus

1 One day at Caesarea Philippi Jesus asked his disciples, "Who do you say I am?" "You are the Christ, the Son of God," Peter answered. Then Jesus began to tell them how he must suffer and die.

2 About a week after Peter's declaration, Jesus took three of the disciples—Peter and James and John—and went up on a mountain with them alone.

3 As Jesus was praying before them, he was transfigured, or changed in appearance. His clothes glistened and became white as the light. His face shone like the sun.

4 Suddenly the disciples saw Elijah and Moses, two of the great men of God of the Old Testament, talking to Jesus!

5 Peter was confused and afraid. He said, "Lord, it is good that we are here. Let us make three booths, one for you and one for Moses and one for Elijah."

6 While Peter was still speaking, a bright cloud overshadowed them. A voice spoke out of the cloud, saying, "This is my beloved Son. Listen to him."

7 Hearing this, the disciples were filled with awe and fell on their faces. Jesus came and touched them, saying, "Get up. Don't be afraid." They saw that Jesus was now alone.

8 As they were coming down the mountain later, Jesus told them, "Don't say anything to anyone about what you saw until the Son of Man is raised from the dead."

9 The disciples asked Jesus, "Then why do the scribes (the teachers of the Jewish law) say that first Elijah must come?"

10 "Elijah does come and he is to restore all things," Jesus answered.

11 "But I tell you that Elijah has already come," Jesus continued, "yet they did not know him and did what they pleased to him."

12 "So also the Son of Man will suffer at their hands," he said. Then the disciples understood that Jesus was talking about John the Baptist.

A Blind Man Sees

1 One sabbath day, Jesus noticed a man who had been blind all his life. The disciples asked him, "Was this man born blind because of his parents' sins or his own sins?"

2 Jesus answered, "Neither this man nor his parents sinned. This has happened so that the work of God might be shown in his life."

3 Jesus spat on the ground and made some mud. He put this on the man's eyes. Then Jesus said to him, "Go and wash in the pool of Siloam."

4 When the man did as Jesus said, he could see! His neighbors were amazed. "Isn't this the man who used to sit and beg?" they asked one another. "Yes, it is I," the man said.

5 He told them his story. Then they took him to the Pharisees, and again he told his story. The Pharisees said, "This Jesus is not from God, for he does not keep the sabbath."

6 But others asked, "How can a sinner do such miracles?" Finally they asked the blind man, "What do you say about the man who opened your eyes?" "The man is a prophet," he said.

7 The Jews still did not believe that the man had really been blind. They sent for his parents and asked, "Is this your son? Was he born blind? How can he now see?"

8 His parents said, "He is our son and he was born blind. But we don't know how he can now see." The Pharisees again said to the man, "We know this Jesus is a sinner."

9 The man replied, "I don't know about that, but I do know that I can now see." They asked him to tell the story again. "Why?" he asked. "Do you want to become his disciples?"

10 The angry Pharisees said, "*You* are his disciple. We are disciples of Moses!" And they threw the man out of the synagogue.

11 Jesus heard what had happened. When he found the man, Jesus asked him, "Do you believe in the Son of Man?" "Who is he?" the man asked in reply.

12 Jesus said, "You have now seen him; in fact he is the one speaking with you." Then the man said, "Lord, I believe!" And he worshiped Jesus.

The Good Samaritan

1 One of the scribes, the teachers of the Jewish law, asked Jesus a question in order to test him.

2 "Teacher," he said, "what must I do to inherit eternal life?" Jesus answered by asking him a question: "What is written in the law? What do *you* think the answer is?"

3 The teacher answered: "'Love the Lord your God with all your heart and soul and strength and mind,' and 'Love your neighbor as yourself.'"

4 "Your answer is correct," Jesus said. "Do this and you will live." But the scribe wanted to make himself look good, so he asked, "Well, who is my neighbor?"

5 Jesus answered with this story: "A man was going down from Jerusalem to Jericho."

6 "On the way some robbers attacked him. They tore off his clothes and beat him. They left the man half dead."

7 "Now a priest happened to come down the same road. When the priest saw the man lying there, he didn't stop. He moved to the other side of the road and went on by."

8 "Then a Levite came along. When he saw the man who had been robbed and beaten, he too passed by on the other side of the road, just as the priest had done."

9 "Finally, a Samaritan came along. When he saw the man lying there he felt pity for him. He stopped and put oil and wine on the man's wounds and bandaged them."

10 "Then he put the man on his donkey and took him to an inn. The Samaritan took care of him that night."

11 "The next morning the Samaritan gave the innkeeper some money and said, 'Please take care of this man. If you spend more than this, I'll repay you when I come back.'"

12 Jesus asked the scribe, "Which of these three acted like a neighbor to the man who was hurt?" The scribe said, "The one who showed mercy." "You go and do the same," Jesus said.

The Lost Son

1 The Pharisees criticized Jesus, saying, "This man welcomes sinners and tax collectors and even eats with them." So Jesus told them this parable.

2 "There was a man with two sons. One day the younger one said, 'Father, give me my share of your property.' So the father divided what he owned between the two sons."

3 "Not long after that, the younger son got all his money together and set off for another country far away. There he wasted all his money in wild living. All his money was gone."

4 "Then a famine came upon that land. The younger son was in need, so he took a job feeding pigs. He was so hungry that he wished he could even eat the food he fed the pigs."

5 "Then he came to his senses. He thought, 'Even my father's workers have food. I'll go back and admit that I've done wrong. Maybe my father will let me be like one of his workers.'"

6 "So he went home. His father saw him from a distance and was filled with pity for his son. He ran to him and threw his arms around him and kissed him."

7 "The son said, 'Father I have sinned against God and against you. I am no longer worthy to be called your son.'"

8 "But the father said to the servants, 'Hurry. Bring the best robe and a ring and sandals for my son, and make a feast. My son was dead and is alive again! He was lost and is found!'"

9 "Now the older son was in the fields at this time. When he heard all the music and dancing, he asked what had happened. When they told him, he was angry and would not go in."

10 "The father came out and pleaded with him. But the older son said, 'Look, I have worked all these years for you and never disobeyed you, but you never gave me a party!'"

11 "'But my brother has come home after wasting your money and you have killed the best calf and held a great celebration for him!'"

12 "The father said, 'My son, you are always here and can have anything you want. But your brother was dead and is alive again. He was lost and is found. It is fitting that we celebrate.'"

Lazarus Is Raised

1 Some friends of Jesus lived in Bethany, about two miles from Jerusalem. They were Mary and Martha, two sisters, and their brother Lazarus.

2 One day Jesus received a message from the sisters. It said: "Lord, the one you love is sick." But Jesus waited for two days before he said to the disciples, "Let's go to Judea."

3 The disciples said, "But just a short time ago the Jews tried to stone you there. Why do you want to go back?" Thomas said, "Well, let us go, too, so that we may die with him."

4 Martha went out to meet Jesus as he neared Bethany. She said, "Lord, if you had only been here, my brother would not have died. But I know even now that God will do whatever you ask."

5 Jesus said to her, "I am the resurrection and the life. He who believes in me will live, even though he dies. Do you believe this?" "Yes," she said. "I believe you are the Son of God."

6 Then Martha called Mary, who fell at Jesus' feet and said, "If you had been here, Lord, my brother would not have died." Jesus was deeply moved by their grief. He cried, too.

7 Then they took him to the cave where Lazarus was buried. Jesus commanded, "Take away the stone." "But Lord," Martha said, "it has been four days. By now there will be a bad smell."

8 Jesus replied, "Didn't I tell you that if you believed, you would see the glory of God?" So they took away the stone.

9 Jesus lifted up his eyes and prayed. "Father, I thank you that you have heard me. I know you always hear me, but I have said this so that these people may believe you have sent me."

10 Then Jesus called out in a loud voice, "Lazarus, come out!"

11 And Lazarus came out, his hands and feet still wrapped with strips of linen and with a cloth around his face! "Take off the grave clothes and let him go," Jesus ordered.

12 Many of those who saw this believed in him. But others reported it to the Pharisees, who called a meeting of the Jewish Council. From that day on they made plans to kill Jesus.

The Ten Lepers

1 On the way to Jerusalem, Jesus and the disciples were passing between Galilee and Samaria.

2 As they entered a village, they were met by ten lepers. The lepers stood at a distance and called with a loud voice, "Jesus, Master, have mercy on us!"

3 Jesus said to the lepers, "Go and show yourselves to the priests." So the lepers started off, and as they went along they were healed!

4 One of them, when he saw that he had been healed, turned around and went back, praising God with a loud voice. He fell at Jesus' feet and thanked him. This man was a Samaritan.

5 Jesus said, "Were there not ten lepers who were healed? Where are the other nine? Was there none but this foreigner who returned to give thanks to God?"

6 Then Jesus said to the Samaritan who had been healed, "Get up and be on your way. Your faith has made you well."

7 On another occasion, Jesus told this parable to some people who thought themselves to be very good and who looked down on other people.

8 "Two men went up to the temple to pray. One was a Pharisee and the other was a tax collector."

9 "The Pharisee stood and prayed like this: 'God, I thank thee that I am not like other men, who steal and do what is wrong—even like this tax collector.'"

10 "'I fast two times every week and I give back to you a tenth of everything I get.'"

11 "But the tax collector would not even lift up his eyes to heaven. He beat himself on the chest and said, 'God, be merciful to me a sinner.'"

12 Jesus said, "I tell you it was the tax collector, not the Pharisee, who went home forgiven. Whoever tries to make himself great will be humbled, but the humble will be exalted."

231

The Rich Young Ruler

1 Jesus had now finished his work in Galilee and had come to Judea, on the other side of the Jordan. The crowds came to him there, and as usual he taught them.

2 Then Jesus set out for Jerusalem. Just about that time, a man ran up and fell on his knees before Jesus. He said, "Good Teacher, what must I do to inherit eternal life?"

3 Jesus said, "Why do you call me good? No one is good but God alone." Then he continued, "You know the commandments: Do not murder. Do not steal. Do not lie. Honor your father and mother. . ."

4 The young man replied, "Teacher, I've obeyed these laws ever since I was just a boy." And Jesus looked at the young man and loved him.

5 But Jesus said, "There is one thing you lack. Go and sell everything you have and give it to the poor—then you will have treasures in heaven. Then come and follow me."

6 When the young man heard this, his face fell. He got up and went away sadly, because he was very rich.

7 Jesus looked around and said, "How hard it will be for those who are rich to enter the kingdom of God!"

8 The disciples were shocked at these words. Jesus added, "It is easier for a camel to go through the eye of a needle than for a rich man to enter the kingdom of God."

9 They were very surprised. "Then who can be saved?" they asked. Jesus looked at them and said, "With men it is impossible, but not with God. For God, all things are possible."

10 Peter said, "We have left everything and followed you."

11 Jesus responded, "Anyone who leaves his home or brothers or sisters or mother or father or children or fields for me and for the gospel will receive much more in this present age."

12 "He will receive a hundred times more houses, brothers, sisters, mothers, children, and fields— along with persecutions—and in the age to come, he will receive eternal life!"

233

Bartimaeus and Zacchaeus

1 Once when Jesus was leaving Jericho, a great crowd was following him. He came upon a blind man named Bartimaeus, who was begging beside the road.

2 When Bartimaeus heard the noise of many people going by, he asked someone, "What's happening?" He was told, "Jesus of Nazareth is passing by."

3 Then Bartimaeus began to cry out, "Jesus, Son of David, have mercy on me!" Those in front said, "Be quiet!" But he only cried louder, "Son of David, have mercy on me!"

4 Jesus stopped and said, "Call him." So they said to Bartimaeus, "Get up! He's calling you!" Bartimaeus threw off his cloak and jumped up and came to Jesus.

5 "What do you want me to do for you?" Jesus asked. Bartimaeus said, "Master, let me receive my sight." "Go your way," Jesus said. "Your faith has made you well."

6 Instantly Bartimaeus could see! He followed Jesus down the road, giving thanks to God. The crowds who saw this also praised God.

7 Another time, Jesus was passing through Jericho. A rich tax collector named Zacchaeus wanted to see Jesus. But he was small and could not see over the crowd.

8 So Zacchaeus ran ahead and climbed up into a sycamore tree beside the road where Jesus was going to pass.

9 When Jesus came to that place, he looked up and said, "Zacchaeus, hurry and come down. I must stay at your house today." So Zacchaeus quickly climbed down, filled with joy.

10 Now Zacchaeus was a chief tax collector and some of the people who saw this complained. They said, "Jesus has gone in to be the guest of a man who is a sinner."

11 In his house, Zacchaeus stood before Jesus and said, "Lord, I will give half of all I have to the poor. If I have cheated anyone, I'll pay him back four times as much."

12 Jesus said to him, "Today salvation has come to this house, since he also is a son of Abraham. For the Son of Man came to seek and save the lost."

Jesus Enters Jerusalem

1 Jesus and his disciples were on their way to Jerusalem. When they reached the Mount of Olives, which is not far from the city, Jesus stopped.

2 He sent two disciples into a nearby village to get a donkey colt. Jesus said, "If anyone asks why you are doing this, say, 'The Lord needs it and will send it back immediately.'"

3 When the disciples entered the village, they found a donkey colt tied at a door. As they untied it, someone standing there asked, "What are you doing, untying that colt?"

4 They answered just as Jesus had instructed and were allowed to take the colt. When they brought it to Jesus, they threw their garments on it. Jesus got on and rode toward Jerusalem.

5 As Jesus rode toward the city, many people spread out their garments on the road ahead of him, and others spread leafy branches which they had cut in the fields.

6 The people were very excited. They shouted, "Hosanna! Blessed is he who comes in the name of the Lord! Blessed is the kingdom of our father David that is coming!"

236

7 Jesus entered the city of Jerusalem in this way. Next, he went to the temple and looked all around. Then, because it was getting late in the day, he went out to Bethany.

8 The next day Jesus returned to Jerusalem. He went again to the temple. This time he began to drive out the people who were buying and selling things there!

9 Jesus overturned the tables of the money-changers and the seats of those who sold pigeons. He would not allow anyone to carry anything through the temple.

10 Jesus said, "Is it not written, 'My house shall be called a house of prayer for all the nations'? But you have made it a den of robbers!"

11 The chief priests and scribes soon heard about this, of course. They were afraid of Jesus because all the people were impressed by his teaching, but they were determined to kill him.

12 Yet they did nothing to Jesus that day. And when evening came, Jesus and his disciples went out of the city unharmed.

The Widow's Gift

1 It was the last week of Jesus' life on earth. He was in Jerusalem, and during the day he taught the people.

2 On this day he was in the temple, and he sat down near the treasury. He watched as the crowds came and put their money into the treasury to help support the temple.

3 He saw many rich people come and put in large amounts of money.

4 But then he noticed a poor woman who came up and put in only two copper coins, which are worth only a penny.

5 Seeing this, he called his disciples to him and said, "This woman has really put in more than all those rich people who are putting money into the treasury."

6 "They gave large sums, and they had much money left. But this woman is very poor. She has given everything she has—her whole living!"

7 Later, as Jesus was leaving the temple, one of the disciples said, "Look, Teacher! What wonderful stones and what a wonderful building!"

8 Jesus said to him, "Do you see these buildings? They will all be torn down. There will not be one stone left on top of another."

9 They went to the Mount of Olives. But James and John, still thinking of what Jesus had said, asked, "When will this happen? What will be the sign that it is about to happen?"

10 Jesus answered, "You will hear of wars, and earthquakes, and famines; and all of these things will happen. Jerusalem will be overrun by the Gentiles. But this is not the end of everything."

11 "You yourselves will be hated and beaten. But you will stand before governors and kings as my witnesses, and you must stand firm to the end."

12 "So be alert; I have told you these things ahead of time. Heaven and earth will pass away, but my words will never pass away."

The Passover Approaches

1 Jesus said to the disciples, "In two days the Passover will be celebrated. At that time the Son of man will be handed over to be crucified."

2 In fact, the chief priests and elders were meeting at the house of Caiaphas, the high priest, to discuss how they could arrest and kill Jesus.

3 However, they were afraid of the people, who liked Jesus very much. So these Jewish leaders agreed, "We will wait until after the feast, so there will not be a riot."

4 But then Judas Iscariot, one of Jesus' own disciples, came to the chief priests with an offer.

5 He asked them, "What will you give me to deliver Jesus to you?" The chief priests were very pleased at this opportunity. They agreed to give Judas thirty pieces of silver.

6 From that moment on, Judas looked for a chance to betray Jesus when the crowds were not around.

7 On the first day of the Feast of Unleavened Bread, the disciples came to Jesus. "Where do you want us to prepare for you to eat the Passover meal?" they asked.

8 Jesus told two of the disciples, Peter and John, what to do and sent them into Jerusalem.

9 When they entered the city, they met a man carrying a jar of water, just as Jesus had said they would. They followed this man to a house, which he entered.

10 The disciples said to the owner of the house, "The Teacher says, 'Where is the room where my disciples and I will eat the Passover meal?'"

11 The owner of the house took them upstairs and showed them a large room which had been furnished and made ready for the Passover.

12 Peter and John took care of everything so that Jesus could eat the Passover meal there with all the disciples that evening. This was the evening when Judas would betray Jesus.

The Last Supper

1 That evening, as the Passover meal was being served, Jesus got up. He took off his outer cloak and wrapped a towel around his waist.

2 He then poured water into a bowl and began to wash the disciples' feet, drying them with the towel at his waist.

3 When he came to Peter, Peter said, "Lord, you shall never wash my feet!" But Jesus replied, "Unless I wash you, you have no part with me."

4 "Then not just my feet, Lord," Peter said. "Wash my hands and my head, too." Jesus said, "A person who has had a bath needs only his feet washed."

5 When he had finished washing their feet, Jesus put his cloak back on and returned to his seat. "Do you understand what I have done for you?" he asked.

6 "You call me 'Teacher' and 'Lord.' Now that I, your Lord and Teacher, have washed your feet, you also should wash one another's feet. I have set an example for you."

7 "No servant is greater than his master, nor is a messenger greater than the one who sent him. Now that you know these things, you will be blessed if you do them."

8 During the meal, Jesus sadly said, "One of you is going to betray me." The disciples stared at one another, wondering whom he meant. Jesus said, "It is he to whom I give this bread."

9 He gave the bread to Judas Iscariot. As soon as Judas took the bread, he got up and went out into the night. The others did not understand why Judas had left. Only Jesus knew.

10 As they ate together, Jesus took some bread. He blessed it and broke it apart and gave it to the disciples. "Take this and eat it," he said. "This is my body."

11 Then he took a cup and gave thanks for it. He gave it to the disciples, who all drank from it. And Jesus said, "This is my blood of the covenant, which is poured out for many."

12 "Truly I will not drink again of the fruit of the vine until I drink it new in the kingdom of God."

Jesus Is Arrested

1 Jesus ate the Passover meal with his disciples in the upper room in Jerusalem. Afterward they sang a hymn. Then they went out to the Mount of Olives—all but Judas.

2 There Jesus said to the disciples, "You will all leave me. But after I am raised up, I will go before you to Galilee."

3 Peter said, "Even if everyone else leaves you, I will not!"

4 Jesus replied, "Truly, this very night before the cock crows twice, you will deny me three times."

5 Then Peter almost shouted, "Even if I must die with you, I will not deny you!" The other disciples said the same thing.

6 When they came to the place called Gethsemane, Jesus said to the disciples, "Wait here while I pray." He took only Peter, James, and John with him.

7 Jesus became very deeply distressed and troubled. He said to the three disciples, "Sorrow has overcome me. Stay here and keep watch."

8 Jesus went on a little farther and fell to the ground. He prayed, "Father, everything is possible for you. Take this cup from me! However, not what I want, but what you want."

9 When he went back to Peter, James, and John, they were asleep. He said to Peter, "Could you not keep watch for one hour? Watch and pray so that you will not fall into temptation!"

10 Again Jesus went away and prayed. And again he found the disciples sleeping. This happened yet a third time. Then Jesus said, "Get up. The hour has come. Here is my betrayer!"

11 Just then Judas came up. With him were men carrying swords and clubs. They had been sent by the Jewish leaders. Judas went at once to Jesus and kissed him.

12 At this signal, the mob grabbed Jesus. Peter drew his sword and struck the high priest's servant, cutting off his ear. The others ran away, leaving Jesus alone with his enemies.

Jesus Before the Sanhedrin

1 After Jesus was arrested in Gethsemane, he was taken to the high priests. All the chief priests and scribes had assembled. This was the Sanhedrin, the Jewish court.

2 Peter followed at a distance. He came right into the courtyard of the high priest. He warmed himself at the fire where the guards were sitting.

3 The counsel wanted to find witnesses who would testify against Jesus so that they could put him to death. But the witnesses' testimony did not agree.

4 Finally two stood up and spoke against Jesus. "We heard him say, 'I will destroy this temple made with hands and in three days I will build another not made with hands.'"

5 The high priest stood up and asked Jesus, "Have you no answer? What is it that these men testify against you?" But Jesus remained silent, giving no answer.

6 The high priest asked, "Are you the Christ, the Son of God?" Jesus said, "I am, and you will see the Son of man sitting at the right hand of God, and coming with the clouds of heaven."

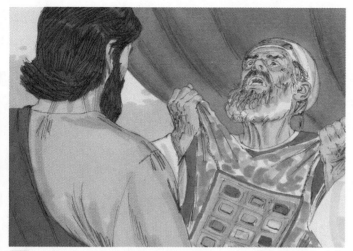

7 The high priest tore his garment and said, "Why do we need other witnesses? You have heard his blasphemy! What is your decision?"

8 They all condemned Jesus as deserving death. Some began to spit on him. Others covered his face and struck him and said, "Prophesy to us, you Christ. Who hit you?"

9 One of the maids of the high priest came into the courtyard. When she saw Peter, she said, "You were with Jesus." Peter said, "I don't know what you are talking about."

10 Then he went to the gateway and the maid saw him again and began to tell bystanders, "This man is one of them." But again Peter denied it.

11 A little later, some bystanders said to Peter, "You must be one of them, for you are a Galilean." Peter began to curse and swear, "I don't know this man of whom you speak."

12 Just then the cock crowed a second time. Suddenly Peter remembered what Jesus had said. And he broke down and cried.

Jesus' Trial Before Pilate

1 Early the next morning after questioning Jesus, the Jewish authorities took him to the palace of Pilate, the Roman governor. They would not go inside for fear of being defiled.

2 So Pilate came out and asked, "What charges do you bring against this man?" The priests said, "If he were not a criminal, we would not have brought him. But we cannot execute anyone."

3 Pilate went back inside the palace and questioned Jesus. "Are you the king of the Jews?" he asked. Jesus answered, "My kingdom is not of this world. It is from another place."

4 "Then you are a king!" said Pilate. Jesus said, "Yes, I am a king. For this reason I came into the world, to testify to the truth." "What is truth?" Pilate asked.

5 He went out and said to the people, "I find no basis for a charge against Jesus. But as is my custom, I will release one prisoner at the Passover. Shall I release 'the king of the Jews'?"

6 The crowd shouted, "No, not him! Give us Barabbas!" (Barabbas was a Jew who had been arrested for taking part in a rebellion.)

7 Then Pilate had Jesus whipped. The soldiers put a crown of thorns on his head and put a scarlet robe on him. They said, "Hail, King of the Jews!" And they slapped his face.

8 Again Pilate said, "Look, I find no fault with this man." When Jesus was brought out wearing the crown of thorns and the scarlet robe, the crowd shouted, "Crucify him! Crucify him!"

9 But Pilate said, "*You* take him and crucify him. I find no basis for a charge against him." The priests said, "Our law says he must die, because he claimed to be the Son of God."

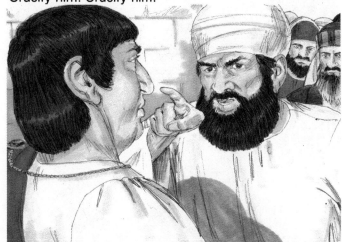

10 Pilate was even more afraid. He tried to set Jesus free, but the priests said, "If you free him, you are no friend of Caesar. Anyone who claims to be a king opposes Caesar."

11 Then Pilate sat on his judgment seat and brought Jesus to him. "Here is your king!" he said to the people. "Take him away," they shouted. "Crucify him!"

12 "Shall I crucify your king?" Pilate asked. The chief priests said, "We have no king but Caesar." So finally Pilate handed Jesus over to be crucified.

The Crucifixion of Jesus

1 So Pilate agreed to crucify Jesus. The soldiers led him back into the palace and mocked him, saying, "Hail, King of the Jews." They struck him on the head and spat on him.

2 Finally, they took off the purple cloak and put Jesus' own clothes back on him. Then they led him out to crucify him.

3 A man named Simon, who was from Cyrene, happened to be passing by at that time. The soldiers made Simon carry Jesus' cross.

4 They brought him to the place called the Skull (Golgotha). There they nailed Jesus to the cross and raised it up. It was about nine o'clock in the morning.

5 The soldiers gambled to see who would get his clothes.

6 On Jesus' cross was a sign giving the charge for which he was crucified: "The King of the Jews." Two robbers were crucified beside him, one on the right and one on the left.

7 The people who passed by made fun of Jesus. They said, "You claimed you would destroy the temple and build it in three days! Save yourself and come down from there!"

8 The chief priests and scribes also mocked him. They said, "He saved others, but he cannot save himself! Let the King of Israel come down from the cross so we can believe in him!"

9 At about twelve o'clock, darkness came over the whole land. It lasted for three hours.

10 Then at about three o'clock, Jesus cried with a loud voice, "My God, my God, why have you forsaken me?" Not long after that, Jesus gave a loud cry and died.

11 Standing far away and watching were Mary Magdalene, Mary the mother of James and Joseph, Salome, and many other women who had come with Jesus from Galilee to Jerusalem.

12 When the centurion who stood facing Jesus saw how he died, he said, "Surely this man was the Son of God!"

Jesus Lives Again

1 Thus Jesus died, nailed to a cross between two robbers.

2 That evening, a man named Joseph of Arimathea went to Pilate, asking for the body of Jesus. Joseph was a rich man who was a disciple of Jesus.

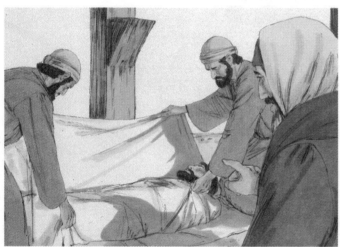

3 With Pilate's permission, Joseph took the body of Jesus down from the cross. He wrapped it in a linen cloth and put it in his own new tomb, which was cut out of rock.

4 The chief priests and Pharisees went to see Pilate, too. They said, "This imposter, while he was alive, said 'I will rise again after three days.'"

5 "We fear his disciples will steal his body and say, 'He has risen from the dead.'" Pilate said, "Take guards and make it secure." So they sealed the tomb and stationed guards.

6 On Sunday morning about dawn, Mary Magdalene and some other women went back to the tomb where Jesus' body had been placed. They had been at the tomb when the stone was put in place.

7 But there was a great earthquake, and an angel came and rolled back the stone and sat upon it. The guards trembled in fear and became like dead men.

8 The angel said to the women, "Don't be afraid. I know you are looking for Jesus who was crucified. He is not here, for he has risen, as he said."

9 "Come and see where he lay," the angel said.

10 Then the angel said, "Go quickly and tell his disciples that he has risen from the dead and that he is going ahead to Galilee. There you will see him."

11 The women left quickly from the tomb, filled with fear and with great joy. They ran to tell his disciples the news.

12 And behold—Jesus met them and greeted them! They fell at his feet and worshiped. "Don't be afraid," Jesus said. "Tell my brothers to go to Galilee and there they will see me."

On the Road to Emmaus

1 Mary Magdalene and the other women told the disciples that Jesus was risen. But the disciples found this news difficult to believe.

2 That very day, two of Jesus' followers were on the road to Emmaus, a village about seven miles from Jerusalem. They were talking about all the things that had happened.

3 As they were talking, Jesus himself came up and walked with them. But the two men did not realize who he was.

4 Jesus asked, "What were you talking about just now?" They stood still, looking sad. "Do you not know what has happened in Jerusalem these past days?"

5 "Our chief priests and rulers delivered up Jesus of Nazareth, a prophet mighty in deed and word before God, to be condemned to death and crucified."

6 "We had hoped that he was the one to save Israel. And besides all this, some women of our group say that they went to the tomb this morning and did not find his body."

7 "They even say they saw a vision of angels, who said that Jesus is alive. Some of our group went to the tomb and found it empty, as the women said, but they did not see him."

8 Jesus said, "Foolish men, why are you so slow to believe all that the prophets have spoken? Wasn't it necessary that the Christ suffer these things and enter into his glory?"

9 And Jesus began to interpret to them all the scriptures from Moses and the prophets concerning himself.

10 When they came to Emmaus, Jesus appeared to be going further. They said, "Stay with us, for it is almost evening." So Jesus went in to stay with them.

11 While they were eating, he took bread, blessed and broke it, and gave it to them. Then they recognized that this was Jesus! That very hour they returned to Jerusalem.

12 There the disciples said to them, "The Lord really has risen! He has appeared to Peter!" Then the two men told what had happened and how they recognized Jesus in the breaking of bread.

The Risen Christ

1 After his resurrection, Jesus appeared to his disciples. Thomas was not there at the time.

2 When they said they had seen the Lord, Thomas replied, "I will not believe unless I see the nail marks in his hands and put my hand into his side."

3 About a week later, the disciples were together and Thomas was with them. Though the doors were locked, Jesus came and stood among them and said, "Peace be with you!"

4 Then he said to Thomas, "Put your finger here; see my hands. Reach out your hand and put it into my side. Stop doubting and believe." Thomas said, "My Lord and my God!"

5 Jesus said, "Because you have seen me, you have believed. Blessed are those who have not seen and yet have believed."

6 Another time, Jesus came to the disciples on a mountain in Galilee. He said, "All authority in heaven and on earth has been given to me. Go therefore and make disciples of all nations."

7 "Baptize them in the name of the Father, the Son, and the Holy Spirit. Teach them to observe all that I have commanded you. I will always be with you, to the end of the age."

8 Again, in Jerusalem, Jesus appeared among the disciples. He asked them for something to eat, and they gave him a piece of broiled fish. He took it and ate before them.

9 Jesus said to them, "I told you while I was still with you that everything written about me in the law of Moses and the prophets and the psalms must be fulfilled."

10 "It is written," he said, "that the Christ should suffer and on the third day rise from the dead, and that repentance and forgiveness should be preached in his name to all nations."

11 "You are witnesses of these things. Behold, I send the promise of my Father upon you. But stay in the city until you receive power from heaven."

12 Then Jesus led them out to Bethany. He lifted up his hands and blessed them, and then he parted from them. They returned to Jerusalem with great joy, praising God.

Waiting for the Holy Spirit

1 During the forty days following his resurrection, Jesus appeared to his disciples from time to time. He spoke to them about the kingdom of God.

2 On one such occasion, Jesus said to the disciples: "Stay in Jerusalem and wait for the gift that my Father has promised. In a few days you will be baptized with the Holy Spirit."

3 The disciples asked, "Lord, are you going to restore the kingdom to Israel now?" Jesus replied, "It is not for you to know the times or dates the Father has set by his own authority."

4 "But you will receive power when the Holy Spirit comes on you," Jesus continued. "You will be my witnesses in Jerusalem, Judea, and Samaria, and to the ends of the earth."

5 After Jesus said this, he was taken up before their very eyes, until a cloud hid him from sight. They were still looking up into the sky when suddenly two angels appeared beside them.

6 The angels said, "Why do you stand looking into the sky? This same Jesus who has been taken from you into heaven will come back in the same way."

7 So the disciples returned to Jerusalem. All the apostles, except Judas, were together. Some women, and Mary the mother of Jesus, and his brothers were with them. They devoted themselves to prayer.

8 Judas, however, was dead. After he had betrayed Jesus, he bought a field with the thirty pieces of silver he received for betraying Jesus. He hanged himself there.

9 So Peter said, "We must choose someone who has been with us from the baptism of Jesus until the time he was taken up from us to be a witness with us of Jesus' resurrection."

10 The believers suggested two men. One was Barsabbas (who was also known as Justus). The other was Matthias.

11 Then they prayed, "Lord, you know what is in everyone's heart. Show us which of these two you have chosen to take over the work of an apostle which Judas once had."

12 Then they drew lots, and the lot fell to Matthias. So Matthias was added to the eleven other apostles in the place of Judas.

The Day of Pentecost

1 When the day of Pentecost, the great Jewish festival, came, Jesus' disciples were all gathered in Jerusalem. It was just ten days since Jesus had gone up into heaven.

2 Suddenly, a sound like a strong wind filled the house where they were sitting. What looked like tongues of fire rested on each of them, and they began to speak in other languages.

3 Because it was a holy day, Jews had come to Jerusalem from all nations. Hearing the noise, a large crowd gathered. They were surprised to hear the apostles speaking their own languages.

4 "Aren't these men Galileans?" they asked. "How can they be talking about the wonders of God in our languages?" But some said, "They have just had too much wine."

5 Then Peter spoke to the crowd: "These men are not drunk. This is what the prophet Joel spoke about: 'In the last days,' God says, 'I will pour out my Spirit and they will prophesy.'"

6 "Listen, Jesus of Nazareth was a man through whom God worked miracles and signs, as you yourselves know. But you had Jesus nailed to a cross. Yet God raised him from the dead!"

7 "We are witnesses that God has raised Jesus to life and has put him at his right hand. And Jesus has poured out the Holy Spirit, as he promised. This is what you see and hear."

8 "You may be sure that God has made Jesus, whom you crucified, both Lord and Christ—the Messiah!"

9 These words deeply affected the crowd. "What shall we do?" they asked Peter and the apostles.

10 Peter answered, "Repent and be baptized in the name of Jesus Christ so that your sins may be forgiven, and you will receive the gift of the Holy Spirit."

11 So those who accepted Peter's message were baptized. About three thousand people were added to the group of believers that very day.

12 The believers spent their time listening to the apostles teach, having fellowship with each other, sharing with those in need, and praying. Their hearts were filled with joy.

Peter and John Heal a Beggar

1 One day Peter and John were going up to the temple at three in the afternoon to pray.

2 At that time a man who had been crippled from birth was being carried to the temple gate called "Beautiful." It was here that he begged from those who were going into the temple.

3 This man saw Peter and John as they were about to enter the temple. He said to them, "Sirs, give me money."

4 Peter said, "Look at us." The man did so, thinking they would give him money. "I have no silver or gold," Peter said, "but what I have I give you. In the name of Jesus of Nazareth, walk!"

5 Peter took the man by his right hand and helped him up. Instantly the man's feet and ankles were healed! He jumped to his feet and began to walk.

6 Then he went with Peter and John into the temple courts, walking and jumping and praising God. The people who saw him were amazed, for they recognized him as the crippled beggar.

7 A crowd ran up to Peter and John and the beggar. "Why do you stare at us?" Peter asked. "Do you think that it is by our own power or godliness that this man walks?"

8 "The God of Abraham has glorified his servant Jesus, whom you handed over to be killed. You rejected the Holy and Righteous One and asked that a murderer be released instead."

9 "But God has raised Jesus from the dead. We are witnesses of this fact. And this beggar was healed by faith in the name of Jesus."

10 "So repent and turn to God, that your sins may be removed and that times of refreshing may come from the Lord, and that he may send the Christ, who has been appointed for you—Jesus."

11 "God said to Abraham, 'Through your offspring all people on earth will be blessed.' When God raised up Jesus, he sent him first to bless you by turning each of you from your wicked ways."

12 As Peter was speaking, the priests and Sadducees came up. They were very upset to hear the apostles saying that Jesus had been raised from the dead. They arrested Peter and John and put them in jail.

The Disciples Share

1 Even though the Jewish leaders warned Peter and John not to teach in the name of Jesus, the believers continued to tell others about Jesus with great courage.

2 All the believers felt very close to one another. Each shared his possessions with the others. There was no one among them who had to do without food or clothing or a place to sleep.

3 From time to time those who owned land or houses would sell them and bring the money to the apostles. The apostles would give some of this money to anyone who needed it.

4 One of the believers was a man from Cyprus whom the apostles called Barnabas (Son of Encouragement). Barnabas was one of those who sold a field and brought the money to the apostles.

5 A man named Ananias also sold a piece of property. But he kept back part of the money and brought the rest to the apostles, as though it were the full amount. His wife, Sapphira, knew about this.

6 Peter said to Ananias, "How is it that Satan has caused you to lie to the Holy Spirit and to keep for yourself some of the money you received for the land?"

7 "You did not have to sell the land. And after you sold it, you could have done whatever you wished with the money. Why did you decide to do this? You have not lied to men but to God."

8 When Ananias heard these words, he fell down and died. All who heard what had happened were afraid. Some young men came and got Ananias's body and buried it.

9 About three hours later, Sapphira, his wife, came in. She did not know what had happened to her husband.

10 Peter asked her, "Tell me, is this the price you and Ananias got for the land?" "Yes," she said, "that is the price."

11 Then Peter said, "How could you agree to test the Lord? Look, the men who have just buried your husband are at the door. They will carry you out, too."

12 Immediately, she fell down before Peter and died. The young men took her body out and buried it beside her husband's. Great fear seized the whole church and all who heard about this.

The Arrest of Stephen

1 Even though the apostles had been beaten for preaching about Jesus, they did not stop talking to people. Thus, the number of disciples continued to increase.

2 But then trouble arose within the church. The Greek-speaking Christians felt that their widows were being neglected when the food was distributed each day to the poor of the church.

3 So the twelve apostles called all the church together. They said, "We apostles must not neglect our preaching in order to pass out the food. You choose seven men to do this work."

4 "They must be men who are full of the Spirit and wisdom. We will put them in charge of passing out the food. And we apostles will spend our time praying and preaching the word of God."

5 The church agreed with this idea. So they chose seven men: Stephen, Philip, Procorus, Nicanor, Timon, Parmenas, and Nicolas. Then the apostles prayed and laid their hands on them.

6 The word of God continued to spread. The number of disciples in Jerusalem grew quickly. Even many of the Jewish priests became obedient to the faith.

7 Now Stephen, who was one of the seven chosen to pass out food to poor Christians, was a man full of God's grace and power. He even performed miracles among the people.

8 However, some Jews from the Synagogue of the Freedmen began to oppose Stephen. They argued with him, but Stephen's wisdom was too much for them.

9 So these Jews secretly arranged for some men to tell lies about Stephen. The men went around saying, "We have heard Stephen saying evil things about Moses and about God."

10 Their lies made the people and the Jewish leaders angry. The leaders seized Stephen and brought him before the Sanhedrin (the Council).

11 Certain false witnesses stood up and said, "We have heard this fellow Stephen say that Jesus of Nazareth will destroy the temple and change the customs which Moses gave us."

12 Everyone sitting in the Sanhedrin stared at Stephen. They saw that his face was like the face of an angel.

The Death of Stephen

1 Certain Jews had spread lies that Stephen spoke evil of the temple and of Moses. Stephen was arrested and brought before the Sanhedrin. "Are these charges true?" the high priest asked.

2 Stephen replied: "God appeared to our father Abraham while he was in Mesopotamia and said to him, 'Leave your country and go to the land I will show you.'"

3 "God sent him to this land where you are now living. But he did not give Abraham any of the land. Instead God promised that his descendants would possess the land."

4 "Abraham is the father of Isaac, who became the father of Jacob. Jacob became the father of the twelve patriarchs. The patriarchs sold their brother Joseph as a slave into Egypt."

5 "But God was with Joseph. He gave Joseph such wisdom that after a time Joseph became a ruler over Egypt. Then he brought his father Jacob and his brothers to live in Egypt."

6 "Many years later, God was ready to fulfill his promise to Abraham. But then a pharaoh who did not remember Joseph oppressed our people. So God chose Moses to free his people."

7 "God made Moses, whom his own people had rejected, their ruler and deliverer. And he gave Moses his commandments to pass on to us. But our fathers refused to obey him."

8 "You people are just like your fathers. You resist the Holy Spirit. They killed the prophets who predicted the coming of the Righteous One—and you have betrayed and murdered Him!"

9 These words made the people in the Sanhedrin furious. Then Stephen looked up to heaven and said, "I see heaven open and the Son of Man standing at the right hand of God!"

10 The people covered their ears and yelled at the top of their voices. They rushed at Stephen and dragged him outside of Jerusalem and began to stone him.

11 As they were stoning him, Stephen prayed, "Lord Jesus, receive my spirit!" Then he fell to his knees and cried out, "Lord, do not hold this sin against them!"

12 Thus Stephen died. The witnesses against Stephen laid their garments at the feet of a young man named Saul. Saul approved of the death of Stephen.

Philip Preaches in Samaria

1 Beginning with the death of Stephen, a young man named Saul tried to destroy the church in Jerusalem. He went to the homes of the believers and dragged them off to prison.

2 Many of the believers in Jerusalem fled to other places in Judea and Samaria. But wherever they went, they preached the word of God.

3 One of those who left Jerusalem at this time was Philip, one of the seven chosen to pass out food to the widows of the church in Jerusalem. He went to preach in a city of Samaria.

4 For some time a man named Simon had practiced sorcery in that city. He amazed all the people of Samaria, and they called him "The Great Power."

5 When Philip arrived, he not only preached but performed miracles. Many people who had been crippled or had evil spirits were healed.

6 The people who heard Philip preach the good news about Jesus Christ believed and were baptized.

7 In fact, even Simon himself believed and was baptized. He followed Philip around everywhere, astonished by the great miracles which Philip performed.

8 The apostles in Jerusalem heard that people in Samaria had accepted the word of God. So they sent Peter and John to them.

9 When they arrived, the two apostles found that the Holy Spirit had not yet come upon any of them. So Peter and John prayed and placed their hands on them, and they received the Holy Spirit.

10 Simon, seeing that the Spirit was given by the laying on of the apostles' hands, offered them money. He said, "Give me this ability so that everyone I lay my hands on may receive the Spirit."

11 Peter replied, "You think you can buy God's gift with money? Your heart is not right before God. Repent of this wickedness." "Pray for me," Simon said, "that the Lord will forgive me."

12 On their way back to Jerusalem, Peter and John preached in the villages of Samaria that they passed through. But Philip was told by an angel to go down to the road to Gaza.

The Ethiopian Traveler

1 Philip was on his way along the road that goes south from Jerusalem through the desert to the town of Gaza. An angel of the Lord had instructed him to go there.

2 On the road Philip met an Ethiopian eunuch. This man was an important official in charge of all the treasury of Candace, queen of the Ethiopians.

3 The Ethiopian eunuch had gone to Jerusalem to worship the Lord. On his way home, he was sitting in his chariot reading from the book of Isaiah the prophet.

4 The Spirit told Philip, "Go to that chariot and stay near it." When Philip went up to it, he heard the man reading Isaiah out loud. So Philip asked, "Do you understand what you are reading?"

5 "How can I," he replied, "unless someone explains it to me?" Then he invited Philip to sit with him in the chariot.

6 The eunuch was reading this passage:
"As a sheep led to the slaughter
or a lamb before its shearer is dumb,
so he opens not his mouth."

7 "In his humiliation justice was
denied him.
Who can describe his generation?
For his life is taken up from the earth."

8 The eunuch asked Philip, "Who is the prophet talking about? Is it about himself or someone else?"

9 Philip began with that passage of Scripture and told the eunuch the good news about Jesus.

10 As they were traveling along, they came to some water. The Ethiopian said, "Look, here is water. Is there any reason why I cannot be baptized?"

11 He ordered the chariot to stop. Then both Philip and the eunuch went down into the water and Philip baptized him.

12 When they came up out of the water, the Spirit of the Lord suddenly took Philip away. The eunuch did not see him again but went on his way rejoicing.

The Conversion of Saul

1 When Stephen was stoned, the witnesses laid their garments at the feet of a man named Saul. Saul began to persecute the church in Jerusalem, throwing both men and women into prison.

2 Saul then asked the high priest for letters to the synagogues in Damascus. He wanted permission to arrest any Christians he found there and to bring them back to Jerusalem.

3 Obtaining this authority, Saul went to Damascus. But when he got near the city, a light from heaven suddenly flashed around him.

4 Saul fell to the ground. He heard a voice say, "Saul, Saul, why do you persecute me?" "Who are you, Lord?" Saul asked. "I am Jesus, whom you are persecuting," the voice replied.

5 "Get up and go into the city," the Lord said. "You will be told what you must do." Now the men who were with Saul heard the sound, but they saw no one. They stood there speechless.

6 When Saul got up from the ground, he could not see. He had to be led by the hand into Damascus. For the next three days, he was blind. He neither ate nor drank anything.

7 In Damascus, there was a disciple named Ananias. The Lord called to him in a vision, "Ananias!" "Yes, Lord," he answered.

8 The Lord said, "Go to the house of Judas on Straight Street and ask for a man named Saul. In a vision, Saul has seen you come and place your hands on him to restore his sight."

9 Ananias replied, "But Lord, I have heard about all the harm this man has done to the believers in Jerusalem. He has come here with authority to arrest all who call on your name."

10 But the Lord said, "Go! I have chosen this man to carry my name before the Gentiles and before the people of Israel. I will show him how much he must suffer for my name."

11 So Ananias went to Saul and placed his hands on him. He said, "Brother Saul, the Lord Jesus, who appeared to you, sent me so that you may see again and be filled with the Holy Spirit."

12 Immediately, Saul was able to see again. He got up and was baptized. After he ate, he regained his strength. Thus did Saul, an enemy of the church, become a servant of Jesus.

Saul Begins to Preach

1 Saul had begun to persecute the church in Jerusalem, beginning with the stoning of Stephen. Then, on the road to Damascus, the Lord appeared to him. The persecutor became a believer!

2 Saul spent several days with the disciples of Christ in Damascus.

3 Right away he began to preach about Jesus in the synagogues of the Jews. "Jesus is the Son of God," he said.

4 All the Jews who heard him were amazed. They asked each other, "Isn't this the man who persecuted the disciples of Jesus in Jerusalem? Didn't he come here to arrest those people?"

5 Yet Saul grew more and more powerful. His proofs that Jesus is the Christ were so strong that the Jews of Damascus did not know how to answer him.

6 Finally, after many days had gone by, the Jews made plans to kill Saul. They kept a close watch on the city gates day and night, hoping to capture him.

7 But Saul found out about their plot. One night his followers lowered him in a basket through an opening in the wall, and Saul escaped from Damascus.

8 He then went to Jerusalem, where he tried to join the disciples. But they were afraid of him. They could not believe that he was a disciple.

9 Then Barnabas helped Saul. He told the apostles how Saul had seen the Lord on his journey. He also told them how Saul had fearlessly preached about Jesus in Damascus.

10 After that, Saul stayed with the disciples and went about Jerusalem, speaking boldly in the name of Jesus. He debated with the Greek-speaking Jews, but they tried to kill him.

11 When the church learned of this, they took Saul down to Caesarea and sent him off to Tarsus, his home town.

12 Then the church throughout Judea, Galilee, and Samaria enjoyed a time of peace. It was strengthened and encouraged by the Holy Spirit. And the number of disciples continued to grow.

Peter Heals Aeneas and Dorcas

1 When the persecution of the church began in Jerusalem, many of the disciples went to other places in Judea and Samaria. Most of the apostles remained in Jerusalem.

2 But Peter traveled about the country preaching. On one occasion he went to visit the saints (as the disciples were called) in Lydda, a town near Joppa.

3 In Lydda, Peter met a man named Aeneas. Aeneas was paralyzed. He had not been able to get out of bed for eight years.

4 Peter said to him, "Aeneas, Jesus Christ heals you. Get up and make up your bed."

5 Immediately Aeneas got up! Everyone living in Lydda and Sharon saw him, and they became believers in Christ.

6 Now, one of the disciples living in nearby Joppa was a woman named Tabitha (which is Dorcas in Greek). She was always doing good and helping the poor.

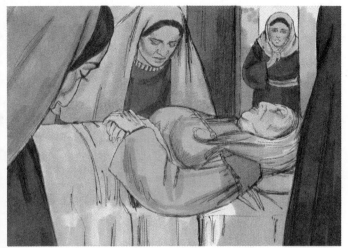

7 While Peter was at Lydda, Dorcas became sick and died. Her friends washed her body and placed it in an upstairs room.

8 When the disciples heard that Peter was in Lydda, they sent two men to him. "Please come to Joppa at once," they urged him.

9 When Peter arrived in Joppa, he went upstairs to the room where Dorcas's body lay. The women there showed Peter the robes and other clothing that she had made while she was alive.

10 Peter then sent everyone out of the room. He got down on his knees and prayed. Then he turned to the dead woman and said, "Tabitha, get up."

11 She opened her eyes, and when she saw Peter she sat up. Peter took her by the hand and helped her to her feet.

12 Then Peter called in the others and presented Dorcas to them alive. When the news of this spread, many people believed in the Lord. Peter remained in Joppa with Simon, a tanner.

Peter and Cornelius

1 In Joppa, Peter had restored to life a woman named Dorcas (Tabitha). Afterwards Peter stayed in Joppa, living in the house of Simon, who was a tanner.

2 About this time an angel appeared to a Gentile named Cornelius, who lived in Caesarea. Cornelius was a Roman centurion who believed in God. The angel told him to send for Peter.

3 At noon the next day, Peter was praying on his roof. He fell into a trance and saw a sheet let down from heaven. It was filled with all kinds of animals and birds and reptiles.

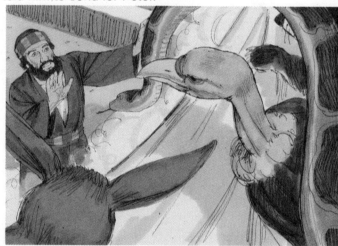

4 A voice said, "Kill and eat." But Peter replied, "I have never eaten anything unclean!" Then the voice said, "Do not call anything unclean that God has made clean." This happened three times.

5 Just as the sheet disappeared back into heaven the third time, the men Cornelius had sent arrived. So Peter went with them and found Cornelius and all his relatives and friends gathered.

6 Peter said to them, "You know that it is against Jewish law for me to visit with Gentiles. But God has shown me that I should not call any man 'unclean.'"

7 "I now understand," Peter said, "that God does not show favoritism. He accepts people from any nation who fear him and do what is right."

8 So Peter preached to these people about Jesus, telling them about the forgiveness of sins for those who believe in Jesus.

9 As he was preaching, the Holy Spirit came on those who listened. They began to speak in tongues and praise God. The Jewish Christians who had come with Peter were amazed.

10 Peter asked, "Can anyone keep these people from being baptized with water? They have received the Holy Spirit just as we have." So Peter ordered them baptized in the name of Jesus Christ.

11 After staying with them a few days, he returned to Jerusalem. There the Jewish Christians criticized him for eating and visiting with Gentiles.

12 Peter told them all that had happened and said, "If God gave them the same gift he gave us, who was I to oppose God?" When they heard this, those who had complained praised God.

Peter Escapes from Herod

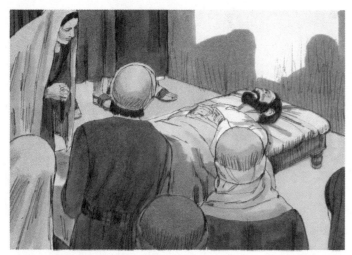

1 King Herod arrested some of the believers in Jerusalem. He had even had the apostle James, the brother of John, put to death with a sword.

2 Because this pleased the Jews, Herod also arrested Peter and put him in prison. This was during the Feast of Unleavened Bread. He intended to put Peter on trial after the Passover.

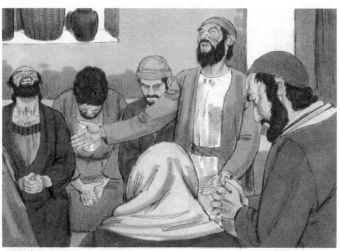

3 While Peter was in prison, chained between two guards, members of the church were praying earnestly for Peter at the house of Mary, the mother of John Mark.

4 The night before the trial, Peter was sleeping between the guards. Suddenly an angel of the Lord woke him. "Quick, get up!" he said. The chains just fell off Peter's wrists.

5 "Follow me," the angel said. So Peter followed him out of the prison. He thought he was dreaming. They passed the guards and came to the iron gate. It opened up by itself!

6 After walking with Peter for a short distance, the angel disappeared. At last Peter realized that the Lord had sent an angel to rescue him from Herod.

7 So Peter went to the house of Mary, the mother of John Mark, where the believers had gathered to pray for him.

8 When Peter knocked, a servant girl named Rhoda came to the door. She recognized Peter's voice and was so excited that she ran to tell the others, forgetting to let Peter in.

9 The other believers said to Rhoda, "You're out of your mind!" But she kept insisting, so they said, "It must be his angel." Peter kept on knocking.

10 When they finally opened the door, they were astonished to see Peter. Peter motioned for them to be quiet and then told them how the Lord had brought him out of prison.

11 The next morning there was an uproar. "What could have happened to Peter?" the people asked. When Peter could not be found, Herod ordered the guards put to death.

12 Later, Herod gave a speech to some people who shouted, "This is the voice of a god, not of a man." Because Herod did not give praise to God, an angel struck him and he died.

The First Journey Begins

■ One day as the prophets and teachers at Antioch worshiped and fasted, the Holy Spirit said: "I have a mission for Barnabas and Saul. Appoint them to do this work."

2 So the leaders of the church prayed and fasted. Then they sent Barnabas and Saul (now called Paul) to preach God's word in various places. John Mark went with them.

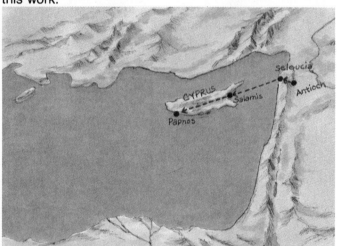

First they sailed to the island of Cyprus, where they preached in the Jewish synagogue at Salamis. Then they went to the other side of the island to the town of Paphos.

4 At Paphos, Sergius Paulus, the governor of Cyprus, wanted to hear them preach. But a Jewish magician named Elymas tried to keep the governor from believing their message.

5 Finally Paul looked straight at Elymas and said: "You are an enemy of all that is right. You turn the Lord's truth into lies. Because of that, the Lord will make you blind."

6 At once a dark mist covered Elymas's eyes. He was blind! He felt around, seeking someone to lead him by the hand. When the governor saw this, he believed.

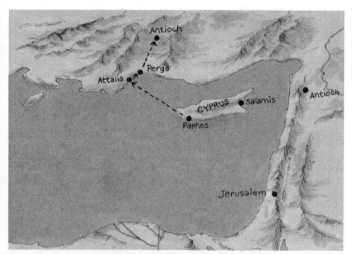

7 Then the missionaries sailed to Perga, where John Mark left them to go back to Jerusalem. Paul and Barnabas went on to Antioch of Pisidia, where Paul was invited to speak to the Jews.

8 First Paul talked about how God had helped Israel in the past. Then he said, "God has made a man named Jesus the Savior of Israel. Yet the people in Jerusalem had him killed."

9 "But God raised Jesus from the dead, and he appeared to many of his disciples. It is through this Jesus that we have forgiveness—everyone who believes in him."

10 As Paul and Barnabas left the synagogue, the people invited them to come back the next week and tell them more. Some even followed after Paul to talk further.

11 The next Sabbath, nearly everyone in the town came to hear them. The Jewish leaders were jealous when they saw the big crowds. So they argued with Paul and insulted him.

12 These Jews persuaded the leaders of the city to run Paul and Barnabas out of town. But God's word continued to spread, and the new believers were filled with joy.

Iconium, Lystra, and Derbe

1 On their first missionary journey, Paul and Barnabas preached on the island of Cyprus and then in Antioch of Pisidia. The Jews of Antioch became jealous and ran them out of town.

2 From Antioch, they went to Iconium. As usual they spoke in the Jewish synagogue, and a large number of Jews and Gentiles became believers. But other Jews stirred up the people against them.

3 Certain people were so angry they planned to stone Paul and Barnabas. But the missionaries learned of the plan, so they went on to Lystra and Derbe. There they continued to preach the good news.

4 At Lystra they met a man who had been a cripple ever since he was born. As the man sat and listened, Paul could tell that he had the faith to be healed. "Stand up on your feet!" Paul said to him.

5 The man jumped up and walked around! When the people saw this, they shouted: "The gods have become men and come down to us!" They wanted to offer sacrifices to Paul and Barnabas.

6 The priest of Zeus brought bulls and flowers so the people could make sacrifices. But Barnabas and Paul cried out, "Why are you doing this? We are only human beings like you!"

7 "We have come here to bring you good news. We want you to turn from the worthless things you call gods to the living God, who made heaven and earth." They barely talked the crowd out of worshiping them.

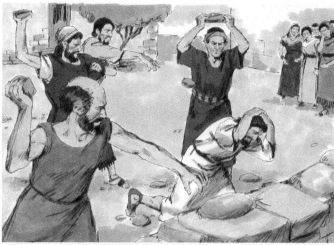

8 But then some Jews came from Antioch of Pisidia and Iconium. They convinced many in the crowd to stone Paul. After the stoning, they dragged him out of town and left him, thinking he was dead.

9 But when the believers gathered around him, Paul got up and went with them back into the town. The next day he and Barnabas went to Derbe. They made many disciples for the Lord there.

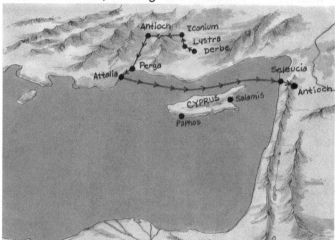

10 Then they went back through the towns where they had preached earlier. They urged the believers to be faithful. "We must pass through many troubles to enter the Kingdom of God," they warned.

11 Paul and Barnabas also appointed elders to guide the new churches. After preaching in Perga, they went to Attalia and boarded a ship for home.

12 When they arrived in Antioch, they called the church together. They reported how God had made it possible for the Gentiles to believe. Thus ended the first of Paul's missionary journeys.

The Second Journey Begins

1 After spending some time with other church leaders in Jerusalem, Paul said to Barnabas, "Let's go back and visit the towns where we preached and see how the believers there are doing."

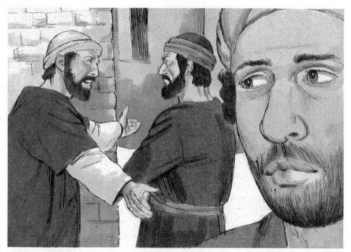

2 Barnabas wanted to take John Mark with them. Paul did not think that this was wise, however, because Mark had left them during the first journey and returned home.

3 Because of this disagreement, Paul and Barnabas decided to separate. Barnabas took Mark and sailed for Cyprus. Paul chose Silas and went through Syria and Cilicia.

4 At Lystra, Paul met a young disciple named Timothy. His mother was a Jewish Christian, but his father was a Greek. Paul wanted Timothy to travel with him, so he circumcised him.

5 They traveled from town to town and encouraged the new Christians. The church grew in faith and numbers every day.

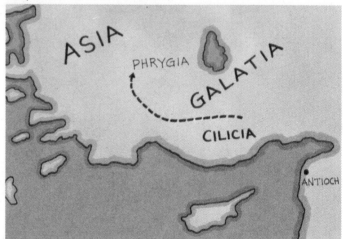

6 Paul and those with him traveled through the region of Phrygia and Galatia. But the Holy Spirit kept them from preaching the word in the province of Asia.

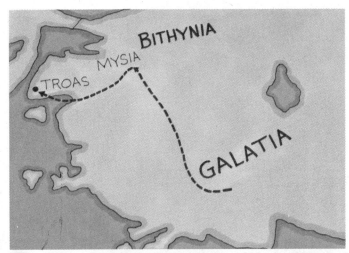

7 When they came to the border of Mysia, they tried to enter Bithynia. But the Spirit of Jesus would not let them. So they passed by Mysia and went down to Troas.

8 During the night, Paul had a vision. He saw a man of Macedonia standing and begging him, "Come over to Macedonia and help us!"

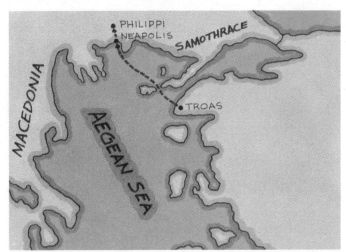

9 Because of Paul's vision, his group concluded that God wanted them to preach in Macedonia. So they made preparations to leave at once.

10 They sailed from Troas to Samothrace and then to Neapolis. From there they went on to the main city of that area of Macedonia—the Roman colony of Philippi.

11 When the Sabbath arrived, they went outside the city to a river, where they found a Jewish place of prayer. They sat down and began to speak to the women who had gathered there.

12 One of these was Lydia. She sold purple cloth and was from Thyatira. The Lord opened her heart and she and all her household were baptized. Lydia invited Paul and his group to stay at her home.

Imprisoned at Philippi

1 Upon receiving the Macedonian vision, Paul and his group went to Philippi. There Lydia and all her household responded to Paul's message and became Christians.

2 One day as Paul was going to the place of prayer, he met a slave girl. She had a spirit by which she predicted the future.

3 This girl followed Paul's group, shouting, "These men are servants of the Most High God. They are telling you the way to be saved." She did this day after day.

4 Finally Paul turned to her and said to the spirit in her, "In the name of Jesus Christ I command you to come out of her." And the spirit left her that very moment.

5 This made her owners very unhappy, because they had made a great deal of money from her fortune telling. So they seized Paul and Silas and dragged them to the marketplace.

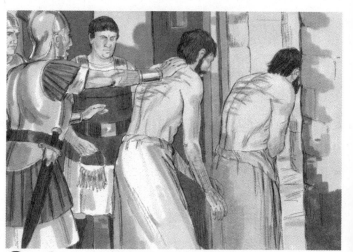

6 There the magistrates of the city had Paul and Silas stripped and beaten and thrown into prison. They told the jailer to guard them carefully.

7 So the jailer put them in an inner cell and fastened their feet in stocks. About midnight, Paul and Silas were praying and singing hymns. The other prisoners were listening.

8 Suddenly there was a violent earthquake! The very foundations of the prison were shaken and all the doors suddenly flew open! Everyone's chains came loose!

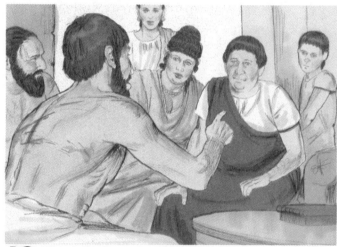

9 When the jailer awoke and saw the open doors, he thought his prisoners had escaped. As he was about to kill himself, Paul shouted, "Don't hurt yourself! We are all here!"

10 The jailer brought Paul and Silas out and asked them, "What must I do to be saved?" They said, "Believe in the Lord Jesus." Then they spoke the word of the Lord to the jailer and his household.

11 The jailer washed their wounds, and then he and his household were baptized. His whole family was filled with joy because they had become believers.

12 The next day the magistrates sent word to release them. But Paul insisted that the magistrates escort them out. Then they encouraged the believers at Lydia's house and left for Thessalonica.

Paul in Athens

1 After preaching in Thessalonica and Berea, Paul went on to Athens. Timothy and Silas stayed for a time in Berea.

2 Paul was saddened to see that Athens was full of idols. On the Sabbath he spoke in the synagogues to the Jews, and every day he talked to the people who came to the marketplace.

3 The Epicurean and Stoic philosophers argued with Paul. Some said, "What is this babbler saying?" Others said, "He seems to be talking about foreign gods."

4 They invited Paul to the Areopagus. "Tell us what this new teaching of yours is," they said. "You are saying some strange things, and we want to know what they mean."

5 So Paul said: "Men of Athens! I see that you are very religious. For as I walked around, I found an altar with the words: TO AN UNKNOWN GOD."

6 "It is this God whom you do not know that I proclaim. The God who made the world and everything in it is the Lord of heaven and earth. He does not live in temples built by men."

7 "He gives all men life and breath and everything else. From one man he made every nation of men. Some of your own poets have said, 'We are his children.'"

8 "Since we are God's children, we should not think that God is like something made from gold or silver or stone—an image made by men."

9 "In the past God overlooked such ignorance," Paul said. "But now he commands all people everywhere to repent."

10 "God has set a day when he will judge the world by the man he has appointed. He has given proof of this by raising him from the dead."

11 When the philosophers heard Paul mention the resurrection of the dead, some laughed at him. But others said, "We want to hear you talk about this again."

12 After Paul left the Areopagus, a few people joined him and believed. One of these was a man named Dionysius, a member of the Areopagus. Another was a woman named Damaris.

Paul Visits Corinth

1 After Paul had preached to the Greek philosophers in Athens, he went on to Corinth. Silas and Timothy had not yet arrived from Berea.

2 At Corinth, Paul met a Jewish couple named Aquila and Priscilla. They had recently come there from Rome.

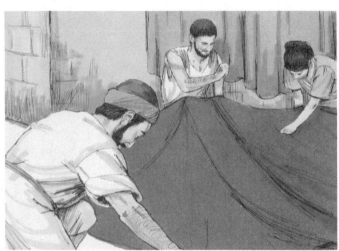

3 Like Paul, Priscilla and Aquila were tentmakers. So Paul stayed with them and worked with them. Every Sabbath he taught in the synagogue, trying to persuade Jews and Greeks.

4 Finally Silas and Timothy came from Berea to Paul in Corinth. After that, Paul preached full time, teaching the Jews that Jesus was the Messiah.

5 But the Jews began to oppose Paul. So Paul said, "Your blood is on your own heads! I am clear of any responsibility. From now on I will go to the Gentiles."

6 Paul then left the synagogue and went next door to the house of Titius Justus, a Gentile who worshiped God.

7 Crispus, who was the ruler of the synagogue, and his entire family believed in the Lord. Many of the Corinthians who heard Paul believed and were baptized.

8 One night, the Lord spoke to Paul in a vision: "Don't be afraid. Keep on speaking. Don't give up. For I am with you."

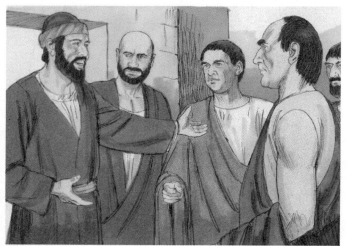

9 "No one is going to harm you, because I have many people in this city." So Paul stayed there for a year and a half, teaching the people of Corinth the word of God.

10 While Gallio was proconsul of Achaia (southern Greece), the Jews had Paul arrested. In court they charged, "This man is persuading people to worship God in ways contrary to the law."

11 Just as Paul was about to speak, Gallio said to the Jews: "If you Jews were complaining about some wrongdoing or crime, it would be right for me to listen to you."

12 "But this is just a question about your own law," he said, "so settle it yourselves. I will not be a judge of such things." So Gallio had the Jews put out of his court.

The Riot in Ephesus

1 Paul left Corinth and traveled in Galatia and Phrygia for a while, strengthening the churches there. Then he went to Ephesus. For two years he preached there. One day some big trouble arose.

2 A man named Demetrius made silver shrines for the goddess Artemis (also called Diana). He called a meeting of all the craftsmen who depended on this business for a living.

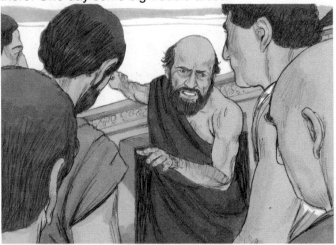

3 Demetrius said to them: "You see how Paul is hurting our business. He tells people that man-made gods are not gods at all. We may lose our jobs and the goddess will not be honored."

4 When the craftsmen heard these words, they were angry. They began shouting: "Great is Artemis of the Ephesians!"

5 Before long, the whole city was in an uproar. A crowd seized Gaius and Aristarchus, two of Paul's friends, and rushed into the outdoor theater with them.

6 Paul wanted to say something to the crowd, but the other believers would not let him. Even some of the officials of the province begged Paul not to go into the theater.

7 The crowd was in confusion. Some people shouted one thing and others something else. Most of them did not even know why they were there.

8 A man named Alexander tried to speak to the crowd. But they recognized that he was a Jew. So they shouted for about two hours: "Great is Artemis of the Ephesians!"

9 Finally the city clerk got the crowd quiet. He said, "People of Ephesus, don't do anything foolish. These men have not robbed a temple or said evil things about our goddess."

10 "If Demetrius and his fellow craftsmen are unhappy, they can take the matter to court. But we are in danger of being charged with rioting because of this."

11 "And if we are, we will have no excuse at all. There is no reason for this commotion."

12 After he said this, the clerk dismissed the assembly and the people went home. Paul and the other Christians were not harmed.

Paul Reaches Jerusalem

1 Paul went back through Macedonia and Greece, encouraging the churches there. Then he sailed back toward Jerusalem. On the way, he stopped for a farewell visit with the Ephesian elders.

2 When he and his helpers reached Tyre, they stayed for a week with the disciples there. These disciples begged Paul not to go to Jerusalem, but Paul's mind was made up.

3 These disciples and their wives and children went with Paul to the beach. They knelt there and prayed. After saying good-bye, Paul and his helpers sailed away.

4 When they arrived in Caesarea, they stayed at the house of Philip the evangelist. After a few days, a prophet named Agabus came down from Judea.

5 Agabus took Paul's belt and tied his own hands and feet with it. He said, "In this way the Jews of Jerusalem will bind the owner of this belt and hand him over to the Gentiles."

6 Hearing this, Paul's helpers and the other believers begged Paul not to go to Jerusalem. But Paul said, "Why are you breaking my heart by asking me not to go?"

7 "I am ready not only to be tied up but also to die in Jerusalem for the name of the Lord Jesus." So they gave up and said, "The Lord's will be done."

8 So Paul and his helpers went on to Jerusalem. The next day they went to see James and the elders of the church. Paul told them what God had done among the Gentiles through him.

9 When they heard these things, they praised God. Then they said to Paul, "There are many Jews who have believed in Jesus. All of them are zealous for the law of Moses."

10 "But they have heard that you teach the Jews who live among the Gentiles to ignore our Jewish customs."

11 "Four men have made a vow. Join them in their purification rites and pay their expenses. Then all will know that you yourself live in obedience to the law."

12 So Paul purified himself with these four men. He also made arrangements for the offering to be made at the temple for each of them when the purification was over.

Paul Is Arrested

1 In Jerusalem, Paul had purified himself along with four other men. When the days of purification were nearly over, some Jews from the province of Asia saw Paul in the temple.

2 They stirred up the crowd and seized Paul. They shouted, "This is the man who teaches against our law and this temple! He has defiled the temple by bringing Greeks into it!"

3 People came running from all directions. They dragged Paul from the temple and shut the gates. Then they began to beat Paul, intending to kill him.

4 When the commander of the Roman troops heard there was trouble, he at once went to the place where they were beating Paul. He arrested Paul and had him bound with two chains.

5 When the commander asked what Paul had done, some shouted one thing and some another. So he ordered Paul taken away. The crowds followed, shouting, "Away with this man!"

6 As they were about to carry him into the barracks, Paul asked the commander if he could speak to the people. Then Paul stood on the steps of the barracks and signaled for quiet.

7 Paul said, "Brothers, listen to my defense." He then told them how he had persecuted the followers of Jesus and how Jesus had appeared to him on the road to Damascus.

8 Then Paul said, "The Lord said to me, 'Go. I will send you to the Gentiles.'" At the mention of Gentiles, the crowd shouted, "Get rid of this man. He is not fit to live."

9 The crowd was shouting and throwing dust into the air. The commander ordered his men to beat Paul in order to find out why the people were so upset with him.

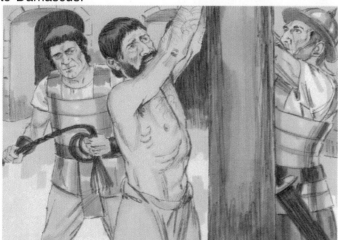

10 The soldiers stretched him out to beat him. But Paul asked the centurion in charge, "Is it legal to whip a Roman citizen who has not even been found guilty?"

11 When the centurion heard this, he went to the commander and reported it. "What are you going to do?" he asked. "This man is a Roman citizen!"

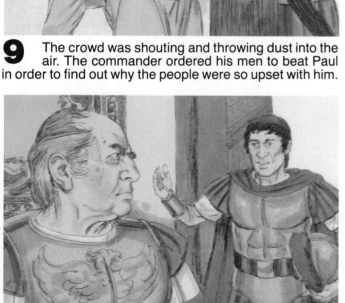

12 The commander asked Paul about this. "Yes, I was born a Roman citizen," Paul replied. So they did not beat him but kept him under arrest until the next day.

A Plot to Murder Paul

1 The Roman commander had arrested Paul because of a riot in the temple. He kept Paul under arrest that night. The next morning he brought Paul before the Jewish Sanhedrin.

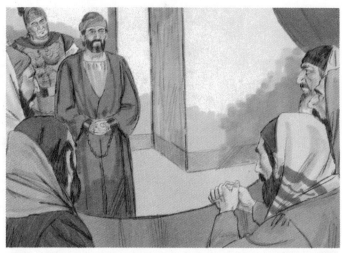

2 Paul knew that some of the Sanhedrin were Pharisees and some were Sadducees. So he said, "Brothers, I am on trial here because of my hope in the resurrection of the dead."

3 This caused an argument between the Pharisees and Sadducees, because the Pharisees believed in the resurrection but the Sadducees did not.

4 Some of the Pharisees stood up and said, "We do not think this man has done anything wrong. What if a spirit or angel has spoken to him?"

5 The argument became so violent that the commander feared Paul would be hurt. He ordered his soldiers to take Paul back to the Roman barracks.

6 The next night the Lord stood near Paul and said, "Have courage! You must testify about me in Rome just as you have in Jerusalem."

7 The next morning some Jews swore an oath that they would not eat or drink again until they had killed Paul. More than forty men were involved in this plot.

8 These men went to the Sanhedrin and asked them to have the Romans bring Paul before the Sanhedrin. They said, "We will set up an ambush and kill Paul before he gets here."

9 But the son of Paul's sister heard of this plot and told the commander of the Roman troops.

10 The Roman commander ordered his soldiers to take Paul to Governor Felix in Caesarea that very night. The commander also wrote a letter to Felix and sent it along.

11 In it he said: "The Jews accuse Paul of crimes, but there is no charge that deserves punishment. However, because of a plot against Paul, I have sent him to you."

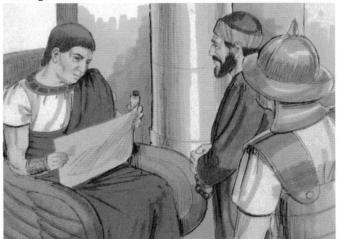

12 The soldiers delivered Paul safely to Governor Felix. When Felix read the letter, he said to Paul, "I will hear your case when your accusers arrive." He kept Paul under guard.

Paul's Trial Before Felix

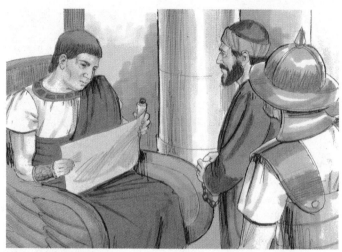

1 The Roman commander had sent Paul to Governor Felix to save him from an ambush. Five days later the high priest and some of the Jewish leaders came to Caesarea.

2 One man presented the case against Paul: "This man is a troublemaker. He stirs up riots among the Jews all over the world. He even dishonored the temple."

3 The other Jewish leaders joined in the accusation. "These things are true!" they said.

4 Then Paul replied, "My accusers did not find me arguing with anyone in the temple or stirring up crowds in their synagogues. They cannot prove these charges against me."

5 "However, I admit that I worship the God of our fathers as a follower of the Way, which they call a sect."

6 "After being away for several years I came to Jerusalem to bring gifts for the poor. I was presenting an offering in the temple when they found me there."

7 "There was no crowd nor any disturbance. But certain Jews from the province of Asia ought to be here. They should make their charges if they have anything against me."

8 "Or these men here should say what crime they found in me when I stood before the Sanhedrin. I only said, 'It is for the resurrection of the dead that I am on trial.'"

9 Governor Felix said, "When the Roman commander comes, I will decide your case." He kept Paul under guard, but he allowed Paul's friends to come and take care of him.

10 A few days later, Felix and his wife Drusilla, who was a Jewish woman, sent for Paul. They listened to Paul as he spoke about faith in Christ Jesus.

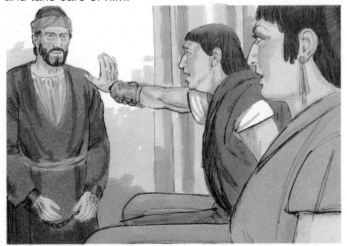

11 Paul preached about righteousness and self-control and the judgment that is coming. Felix became afraid and said, "That's enough for now. At a convenient time I will send for you."

12 Felix hoped that Paul would offer him a bribe, so he talked to Paul often. When Felix was replaced by a new governor named Festus, he left Paul in prison as a favor to the Jewish leaders.

Paul Before Festus and Agrippa

1 About two weeks after Festus replaced Felix as governor, Paul's enemies presented their case against Paul to Festus. They made many charges which they could not prove.

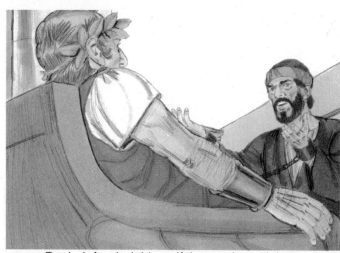

2 Paul defended himself by saying, "I have done nothing wrong against the law of the Jews or against the temple or against Caesar."

3 Festus wanted to do the Jewish leaders a favor. He asked Paul, "Are you willing to go up to Jerusalem and stand trial before me there on these charges?"

4 Paul answered, "I am now standing before Caesar's court, where I ought to be tried. No one has the right to hand me over to the Jews. I appeal to Caesar!"

5 After Festus talked this over with his council, he said, "You have appealed to Caesar. To Caesar you will go!"

6 A few days later King Agrippa came with his wife Bernice to Caesarea to greet Governor Festus. When Agrippa heard about Paul, he said, "I would like to hear this man myself."

7 So the next day Festus brought Paul in before Agrippa and Bernice and all the important men of the city. Agrippa gave Paul permission to speak.

8 Paul said, "I am only saying what the prophets predicted—that the Christ would suffer and rise from the dead and proclaim light to the Jews and Gentiles."

9 At this point Festus interrupted. "Paul, you are out of your mind!" he shouted. "Your great learning is driving you insane!"

10 "I am not insane, most excellent Festus," Paul replied. "What I am saying is true." Then to King Agrippa Paul said, "Do you believe the prophets? I know you do."

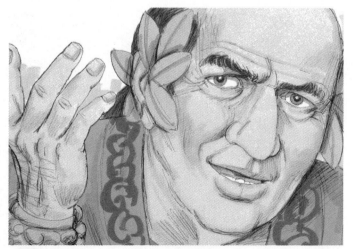

11 Agrippa said, "Do you think that in such a short time you can make me a Christian?" Paul said, "I pray that not only you but all who are here may become what I am!"

12 As they were leaving, Agrippa said to Festus, "If this man had not appealed to Caesar, he could have been set free."

Paul Sails for Rome

1 Because Paul had appealed to Caesar, he was handed over to a centurion, along with other prisoners. The centurion put Paul and the other prisoners on a ship and set sail.

2 They sailed first to Sidon and then along the coast of Cilicia and Pamphylia, landing at Myra in Lycia (in what is now part of Turkey). There they all boarded a ship sailing for Italy.

3 They made slow headway for many days. Finally they reached a town called Fair Havens on Crete. Sailing had already become dangerous, because it was the season for storms.

4 Paul warned them: "Men, I can see that our voyage is going to be disastrous. It will bring great loss to the ship and cargo, and to our own lives also."

5 But the centurion did not listen to Paul. Instead he followed the advice of the pilot and the ship's owner. They set sail again, hoping to spend the winter in Phoenix.

6 Before long, a wind like a hurricane, called a "Northeaster," swept down from Crete. The ship was caught by the storm and was driven along helplessly.

7 As they passed the shelter of a small island they were able to pull the lifeboat on board and tie it down. Then they passed ropes under the ship itself to hold it together.

8 They took such a violent battering from the storm that the next day they began to throw the cargo overboard.

9 On the third day, they threw the ship's tackle overboard. They had not seen the sun or the stars for many days. Finally they gave up all hope of being saved.

10 They had gone without food for a long time. So Paul said: "Men, you should have taken my advice not to sail from Crete. Then you would have been spared this."

11 "But now keep up your courage. Last night an angel of God said to me, 'Do not be afraid, Paul. You must stand trial before Caesar. God will spare everyone on board the ship.'"

12 "So keep up your courage. I have faith in God that it will happen just as he told me. Nevertheless, we will run aground on some island."

Shipwreck on Malta

1 The ship carrying Paul and the other prisoners to Italy was caught in a terrible storm.

2 About midnight on the fourteenth day, the sailors sensed that land was nearby. When they first measured the water, it was a hundred and twenty feet deep.

3 A short time later they measured it again. Now it was just ninety feet deep. They were afraid they would be thrown against rocks, so they dropped four anchors and prayed.

4 Some of the sailors attempted to escape from the ship. They pretended they were going to lower some anchors. But in fact they were trying to lower the lifeboat.

5 Paul said to the Roman centurion, "Unless these men stay with the ship, you cannot be saved!" So the soldiers cut the ropes that held the lifeboat and let it fall away.

6 Just before dawn Paul urged them all to eat. "You have gone without food for fourteen days. I urge you now to eat. You need the strength! Not one of you will be harmed."

7 After he said this, he took some bread and gave thanks to God in front of them all. Then he broke it and began to eat. They were all encouraged and ate some food themselves.

8 When daylight came, they could not recognize the land, but they saw a bay with a sandy beach. They decided to run the ship aground on the beach if they could.

9 They cut loose the anchors and untied the ropes that held the rudders. Then they raised the foresail to the wind and headed for the beach.

10 But the ship struck a sandbar and ran aground. The bow was stuck and would not move, and the stern was being broken to pieces by the pounding of the waves.

11 The soldiers intended to kill the prisoners to prevent any of them from escaping. But the centurion wanted to spare Paul's life and kept them from carrying out their plan.

12 He ordered, "If you can swim, swim for shore now! If you cannot swim, hold to boards or pieces of the ship!" In this way everyone was able to get to the shore safely.

From Malta to Rome

1 The ship taking Paul and other prisoners to Italy had been wrecked on the island of Malta. The islanders were kind and built a fire to warm them.

2 As Paul was putting some wood on the fire, a poisonous snake came out and bit him on the hand. The islanders saw the snake hanging from Paul's hand.

3 They said, "This man must be a murderer. He escaped the sea, but Justice will not let him live." But when Paul did not get sick or die, they said, "He must be a god!"

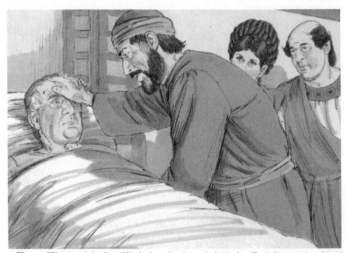

4 The chief official of the island, Publius, invited them to his house for a few days. While there, Paul healed the father of Publius, who was sick with a fever.

5 Then the rest of the sick on the island came and were cured. The people honored Paul in many ways. After three months, they gave the shipwrecked men the supplies they needed to sail on.

6 Finally Paul reached Rome. After three days, he called together the leaders of the Jews. He said: "My brothers, I have done nothing against our people or our customs."

7 "But I was arrested in Jerusalem and turned over to the Romans. They did not find me guilty of any crime deserving death and wanted to release me. But the Jews objected."

8 "So I was forced to appeal to Caesar. Thus I asked to see you and talk to you. It is because of the hope of Israel that I am bound with this chain."

9 The Jews replied, "We have not had any bad reports about you. But we know that people everywhere are talking against the Christians. We want to know what your views are."

10 So on a certain day many of the Jews came to where Paul was staying. All day he tried to convince them about Jesus from the Law of Moses and from the Prophets.

11 Some believed but others would not. Finally Paul said to them, "I want you to know that God's salvation has been sent to the Gentiles, and they will listen."

12 For two whole years Paul stayed in his own rented house in Rome. He welcomed all who came to see him. He boldly preached about the kingdom of God and the Lord Jesus Christ.

Paul's Last Days

1 When the Book of Acts closed, Paul had been a prisoner in Rome for two years. Apparently Paul was released and continued to travel and preach.

2 On his way to Macedonia, Paul left Timothy in Ephesus. "Stay here and command certain people not to teach false doctrines any longer," he instructed Timothy.

3 Paul also left Titus in Crete. He said to Titus, "Straighten out what is unfinished and appoint elders in every town."

4 When Paul wrote to Timothy the second time, he was in prison again. "Do not be ashamed of me, his prisoner," Paul wrote. "Join me in suffering for the gospel of God."

5 "I was appointed an apostle and teacher of this gospel. That is why I am suffering as I am. Yet I am not ashamed, because I know whom I have believed!"

6 "My son, be strong in the grace that is in Christ Jesus. Entrust the things you have heard me say in the presence of many witnesses to reliable men who can teach them to others."

7 "Flee evil desires and pursue righteousness, faith, love and peace along with those who call on the Lord out of a pure heart."

8 "Preach the word. Correct, rebuke, and encourage—with great patience and careful instruction. Endure hardship, do the work of an evangelist, discharge all the duties of your ministry."

9 "The time has come for my departure. I have fought the good fight. I have finished the race. I have kept the faith."

10 "Now there is in store for me a crown of righteousness, which the Lord will award to me on that day, and not only to me but to all who haved longed for his appearing."

11 "At my first defense no one came to my support, but everyone deserted me. Yet the Lord stood at my side and gave me strength so that the message might be fully proclaimed!"

12 "And I was delivered from the lion's mouth! The Lord will rescue me from every evil attack and bring me safely to his heavenly kingdom! To him be glory for ever and ever. Amen."

The Letters of James and John

1 Among the writings in the New Testament are letters written by James and by John.

2 James stressed the importance of good deeds: "What good is it, my brothers, if a man claims to have faith but has no good deeds? Can such a faith save him?"

3 "Suppose a brother or sister is without clothes and daily food and one of you says to him, 'Go. I wish you well. Keep warm and well fed.'"

4 "If you do not give him what he needs, what good are your words? In the same way, faith by itself, if it is not accompanied by action, is dead."

5 "Was not Abraham considered righteous for what he did when he offered his son Isaac on the altar? His faith was made complete by what he did."

6 John emphasized love: "Anyone who claims to be in the light but hates his brother is still in the darkness. Whoever loves his brother lives in the light."

7 "This is the message you heard from the beginning: We should love one another. Do not be like Cain, who murdered his brother. Anyone who hates his brother is a murderer."

8 "This is how we know what love is: Jesus Christ laid down his life for us. And we ought to lay down our lives for our brothers."

9 "If anyone has possessions and sees his brother in need but has no pity on him, how can the love of God be in him? Let us not just talk about love but really show love!"

10 "Dear friends, love comes from God. Everyone who loves has been born of God and knows God. Whoever does not love does not know God, because God is love."

11 "This is how God showed his love among us: He sent his one and only Son into the world that we might live through him! If God so loved us, we also ought to love one another."

12 "We love because he first loved us. If anyone says 'I love God,' yet hates his brother, he is a liar! Whoever loves God must also love his brother."

The Revelation of John

1 John had been exiled to a small island called Patmos because he preached the word of God. One day God sent an angel to show John what must soon take place.

2 A voice said, "Write down what you see and send it to the seven churches: to Ephesus, Smyrna, Pergamum, Thyatira, Sardis, Philadelphia, and Laodicea."

3 John wrote these words of the Lord to the church in Smyrna: "Do not be afraid of what you are about to suffer. Be faithful even unto death and I will give you the crown of life."

4 Then John saw God on his throne and the Lamb of God beside him. He was shown many scenes of the destruction of the earth and of the people on earth who do evil things.

5 Then John saw a woman give birth to a baby boy who was to be the ruler of the world. A great red dragon (Satan) tried to destroy the baby, but it was taken to safety in heaven.

6 Then the dragon chased the woman, but she escaped. So the dragon made war against the rest of her children—the people who keep God's commandments and believe in Jesus.

7 A great beast came up out of the sea. The dragon gave the beast his power and authority. The beast spoke evil against God and made war against God's people.

8 Then the beast and his armies fought with the armies of heaven. The beast was captured and thrown into the lake of fire, and his army was destroyed. Satan was put in prison.

9 After a thousand years, Satan was freed. Again he tried to destroy God's people. This time he was thrown into the lake of fire, to be punished with the beast forever.

10 Then the dead were judged before God in heaven. Each was judged by what he had done. If his name was not in the Lamb's book of life, he was thrown into the lake of fire.

11 Then John saw the Holy City, the new Jerusalem, come down from heaven. In it was the throne of God and of the Lamb. The river of life flowed through the middle of the city.

12 A voice said, "Now God will live with men. He will wipe every tear from their eyes! There will be no more death or crying or pain, for the former things have passed away."